To Mark –
Enjoy my story
Maranatha!
Arthur Birkby

DIG UP
MY GOLD

BUT I WON'T SAY WHERE IT'S BURIED

Arthur Birkby

TATE PUBLISHING, LLC

What Others are Saying...

The title, "Dig Up My Gold, But I Won't Say Where It's Buried," reflects on the sometimes subtle, but always entertaining, humor of its author. I came to know it in battle when his spirits were at their lowest, and in his joy at its highest when he was seated at a pipe organ or piano.

His introductory greeting to the Intelligence Section (where I first met him) was, "Feed me, I'm hungry!" which made us all roar with laughter. Of course, he knew we had no food. In a few moments we stopped laughing as a Buzz Bomb engine fell silent, and the missile plummeted to earth.

Dino Argentini,
S/Sgt, I & R, 3rd Bn.,
289th Inf. Reg., 75th Div.

An excellently written life story with subtle undertones of the life and times of the early 20th century by a gifted musician with an exceptional recollection of events, and a magnificent command of the English language.

Lester M. Zinser
Former Associate Professor,
Western Michigan University.
Retired Atmospheric Research Pilot, NCAR

There is one major problem with Arthur Birkby's autobiography: it ends too soon! I have known Arthur for so long, but did not realize how little I knew of his very interesting early life and his military experiences in Europe. This book is very interesting, with lots of humor and adventure. Biography is not the type of reading in which I usually engage; but this one was well worth the effort.

Bill Banister

This book is delightfully filled with real life experiences. The humor is tactful and told in such a way that makes the reader laugh and enjoy the events described. This book also has historical value in the relating of his experiences of World War II. It's just good reading, told in honest fashion.

Living these events through Arthur's eyes is like taking a trip back into America's past. You will identify with Arthur's "strange" family and be reminded of your own "strange" family. Arthur's portrayal of his family's uniqueness is often very funny, and will give the reader a sense of family pride as he reads of the author's fondness and love for many persons mentioned in the book. It seems as if I know Uncle Bert, Cousin Robert, and Uncle Sylvester, and have made them part of my own life. Being a friend of the author, I can visualize him and hear his voice in each of his stories. You're going to like this book!

Rev. Don Stephens, Pastor
Keizer Community Church, Keizer, Oregon

Contents

Preface 7

1. Grampop 9
2. Uncle Bert 17
3. "Cousin" Robert 35
4. Hub and Dad 49
5. Unrivaled Thrift 57
6. "Uncle" Sylvester. 65
7. Closet Skeletons. 71
8. The Farm 81
9. Early Development 87
10. Future Inklings. 103
11. Hard Times 119
12. The Cadet 127
13. The Call 133
14. Finance. 141
15. Subway Commandos 145
16. Missed Chances 155
17. This is It! 159
18. Civilization. 169
19. A Different Weapon 175
20. Wales 185
21. To the Continent. 195
22. Contact at Last 201
23. Smell of Death 211
24. Going South 227

25. Rhine Crossing. 233
26. End in Sight 241
27. Occupation. 245
28. Biding our Time. 251
29. Military Police 261
30. Homeward Bound 275

Preface

My uncle was knocked twice from a multistory building, and survived. Another uncle placed a chair at the top of the stairs to prevent ghosts from entering his bedroom at night. A soldier in an army tank turret cocked his loaded .50-caliber machine gun and aimed it at me. My grandfather bit off the head of a live mouse on a dare. My cousin operated a bordello. Another cousin was sent to reform school. While on a trolley car, my step grandfather put his hand down a young woman's dress and massaged her bosom.

The above true incidents are among many with which I have regaled my friends in conversation. All are firsthand accounts of events I have experienced myself, or about people I knew personally; and they are the kinds of anecdotes that one is unlikely to invent.

More than once my listeners have told me that I ought to write a book. While I was a university professor in Laramie, Wyoming, I related some of these stories to my pastor and his wife. They were especially titillated by the narrative about my grandmother's hidden gold; and suggested that, were I to write a book, this incident could provide an engaging title. Hence, it is!

Chapter 1

Grampop

"Grampop" was the oldest person I knew when I was a little kid in the 1920's. To this day, I don't know why this step grandfather remains so vividly in my mind. He was not especially influential in my life, but he was an interesting character.

He came alone from Germany at the age of twelve in the year Lincoln was assassinated, crossing the Atlantic on a sailing ship. The passage was stormy and required three months. He related how frightening it was to be in a ship that was hurtled viciously by wind and wave, and how the passengers were certain the ship would not survive the storms.

The ship finally reached port safely, and Grampop settled in Camden, New Jersey, where he learned to make hand-rolled cigars. He worked among a group of Spanish-speaking Cubans, and subsequently became fluent in Spanish as well as English.

To relieve the boredom of stripping, sorting, and rolling tobacco leaves for quality cigars, employees took turns reading aloud to the others while they were working at their craft. I well remember Grampop's telling me about books such as *Don Quixote* and *Les Miserables* that were among those read to the employees. Grampop remained in the tobacco business and ultimately owned his own factory and

retail store. It became a prosperous venture that supported full-time cigar-makers and a fleet of trucks
for distributing their products to stores throughout
southern New Jersey.

While he was at the height of his success he
met and married my grandmother, whose husband
(my real grandfather) died in his forties of heart failure. My real grandfather, whom I had never met, was
also German, and was a cabinet-maker by trade. I
only heard a couple of anecdotes about him, such
as his biting off the head of a live mouse on a dare,
and his nearly severing his foot from his ankle while
chopping wood for the kitchen stove.

*Author's maternal grandparents, Johann and Anna
Wakker, and Uncle Alphonse (center), c. 1893*

But back to Grampop the cigar-maker: He was an avowed atheist and socialist, and was not reluctant to try to persuade others to his views. When Eugene Debs, who was the socialist candidate for President of the United States on numerous occasions, attended the party's national convention in Chicago, Grampop went there to give him support and to contribute to his campaign. I asked Grampop why he always voted socialist, knowing that his candidate would not win. As young as I was, it did not occur to me that anyone would knowingly vote for someone who might lose an election.

Grampop and Grammom lived only two houses from us in West Collingswood, New Jersey; so we saw each other constantly, and always had a good relationship between us. Grampop would visit us frequently, and discuss politics and religion with my father. He told my father that if he, Grampop, were ever to repent and say he was a Christian while on his deathbed, everyone was to know that he had lost his mind.

When my mother would send me to Sunday school, Grampop said that I would be better off if I were to go outside and enjoy the fresh air; to which my mother replied, "If you want to raise your kids to be heathens, go right ahead; but don't tell me how to raise my child!"

In summer, some of the kids in our neighborhood would go barefooted outside, and I wanted to do the same, but my mother forbade it. Grampop said that soldiers in the German army went barefooted in the morning dew, and that it was good for their health. This seemed like a good argument to me, but my mother was unaffected by Grampop's advice.

Grampop was regarded for a number of years as a tycoon in the cigar business. He trusted everyone; but subsequently, mismanagement and unscrupulous employees' stealing from the company caused its ultimate demise.

Four of his five sons worked for him as cigar makers, and when the business went under, one of them salvaged what little remained by running a little hole-in-the-wall tobacco store. Grampop came in every day to make cigars to help keep his son's business intact, and it also gave him something to do. With his advancing years, his attention to care and detail in rolling cigars had diminished. As a result, his son would not put Grampop's cigars on the market. They were his to keep, and he shared them with his smoking acquaintances.

On one occasion my father was smoking a Grampop original, and the smell was horrible. The old man had wrapped an apple core in the cigar to give it a fruity flavor, but the taste and aroma of burning apple was less desirable than intended. At another time, my father was smoking a Grampop special while driving my mother and me in our car. After a few minutes, he thought that the car had an electrical short circuit, or that perhaps the emergency brake was on because of a terrible odor. He soon discovered that the cigar was the source of the problem. Upon examining it and taking it apart, it was found to contain rubber bands.

There is no record of Grampop's ever seeing a doctor or dentist, or going to a hospital, but he lived into his nineties. I recall his having a tooth break off, leaving a sharp, uneven biting surface. To eliminate the sharp edge, he used a coarse rasp to grind away the rough edge. As the years went on, he lost most of his teeth, swallowing them without being aware of it.

Even as an old man he had an eye for the ladies. I saw him sitting in a lawn chair in his back yard one summer day, and the young woman next door was in her yard, wearing a sun suit consisting of shorts and bra. He ogled her intently, and while leaning over to get a better view, fell out of the chair. There was also the incident when he was with Grammom on a bus. The bus driver made an emergency stop, applying the brakes suddenly. Several people including Grammom were thrown from their seats. A young, buxom girl who was in the seat next to them was also thrown to the floor. Grampop stooped down, slipped his hand down the front of her dress, and massaging her bosom, asked, "Are you hurt, girl?" He always addressed anyone younger than himself as either "girl" or "boy." Meanwhile, Grammom was lying on the floor, only mildly injured, but received none of his attention. She told me when she arrived home, "I could kill that old Teufel (devil)!"

Anna and Franz Hartmann
("Grammom" and Grampop"), circa 1922

I wince when I recall the time my father took my mother and me, Grammom and Grampop, and a husband and wife from next door to Armstrong Cork where my father worked. We toured the plant to see how the cork was processed from the time it was bark from a tree until it emerged as corkboard used for insulating walls, refrigerators, floors, pipes, and many other things requiring light, porous covering. We then saw the huge machine shop over which my father was superintendent. Many of the machines such as lathes, shapers, planers, saws, and the like, were in operation. I was only a little boy at the time, and we were watching a mechanic at a milling machine. The machine consisted of a steel table that moved back and forth under a rotating saw-toothed wheel. Grampop, without saying a word, picked me up and put me on the moving table, which was about to transport me under the cutting wheel. A split second later, my father snatched me from the table, preventing me from being sawn asunder. I recall the women present, Mother, Grammom, and the neighbor, shrieking in horror at the close call. Grampop showed no distress at what had happened, but merely said that he wanted to give me a ride, as though it were an amusement park attraction.

Grammom, Grampop, and author, c. 1926

Both Grampop and Grammom were profane when they became angry, using "hell," "damn," and invoking God's name in vain on occasion. Grampop told me that, when I became older, I would be privileged to say more than I was allowed as a child. I looked forward to the time when it would be all right for me to swear with impunity. My mother, of course, made it clear that bad words of any kind were forbidden. Frequently my childhood friends used the common expression, "Yer darn tootin," which meant, "You're right," or "I agree." I asked Mother if I could say "Yer darn tootin," and she allowed me to say, "Yer tootin,'" omitting the expletive, "darn." Somehow, such abridgement lacked the full impact of the real thing.

Some kids I knew referred to their fathers as "Pop," rather than "Dad," and I read newspaper comic strips in which "Pop" was used to address one's father. Whether Mother regarded "Pop" as disrespectful or too chummy, I don't know, but she did not want me to use that designation. I asked my father if he would let me call him "Pop," and he readily agreed. Somehow it gave me a feeling of closer relationship with him, and this was important to me because of our spending so little time together.

Chapter 2

Uncle Bert

S oon after Franklin Roosevelt became President, with the end of the gold standard, everyone was required to turn in to the government any gold in his possession. Although she no longer had financial resources from Grampop, his business having failed, Grammom still had some savings in gold coins that she had hidden in a metal box in her back yard. She was always asking my father to do favors for her, since he was family, and lived only two houses away. She didn't want the neighbors to know about the buried gold, so she asked my father to come over at midnight when the neighbors were presumably asleep. As requested, he went to her house with a spade and a flashlight. They went into the yard, and when he asked her where the gold was hidden, she refused to tell him. She asked, "Do you think me a fool? I don't tell anybody where my gold is!"

My father said that he wasn't about to dig up the whole yard until he found it, and turned to leave. Recognizing the unreasonableness of her request, she relented and told him where the box was located.

Grammom had four children, two having been born in Germany, one of which died as an infant. The other two, my mother and her brother, Albert, were born in Albany, New York. Albert, or Uncle Bert, as I called him, was an unwanted child. He and his father were always arguing about stupid, inconsequential topics such as whether movie actors were moral people. His father said that they were evil, and Albert defended show people as having hearts of gold. His father also insisted that the cowboy actors were actually killed when depicted as being shot. He refused to believe that what was seen on the screen could be created without actually happening. As I reflect on situations involving Uncle Bert—some of which are humorous and some sad—I feel that he was more to be pitied than censured. His father's resenting his ever being born was bound to have an adverse effect on his life.

Author's Uncle Alphonse, mother,
and Uncle "Bert," c. 1900

Uncle Bert was two years younger than my mother, and was always the underdog in his relationship with her. My grandfather had been Roman Catholic and Grammom was reared as a Lutheran. When my mother reached the age of 14 she was, as Lutheran practice required, confirmed. Albert was too young for confirmation; but he raised such a fuss at having to wait to be confirmed alone, that the pastor agreed to allow him to attend catechetical class with his sister so that they could be confirmed together. All church services and ceremonies were conducted in German. Living with her parents, who spoke German exclusively at home, my mother became fluent in speaking, reading, and writing the language. Albert, on the other hand, never learned the language, and was constantly berated by his father for speaking English when addressed in German. My mother successfully learned the catechism, but Albert faked his way, mumbling the answers when the pastor asked him to recite. Despite the difference in the learning achievement between Uncle Bert and my mother, the pastor

Uncle Bert and sister (author's mother) on confirmation day, c 1912

confirmed both of them around 1912.

People who rarely attend church sometimes go at Easter and Christmas. Grammom went to church only on Good Friday. My mother always accompanied her, and I had to go along with them. My mother, being fluent in German, felt at home, sing-

ing the hymns and listening to the sermon. I had not yet become familiar with the language, and sitting through three hours—the usual length of Good Friday services—bored me to death.

Unbelieving Grampop, of course, did not go with us. Grammom said that she made bacon sandwiches

Author's mother, age 18

for his lunch, since he would be home alone. My mother remonstrated Grammom for giving the old man meat instead of fish on Good Friday. Although Lutheran doctrine did not require abstinence from eating meat on Fridays, as did Roman Catholicism, my mother always held her own private doctrinal stance, that Good Friday was such a unique occurrence in the church calendar, that eating meat other than fish was a most serious offence. I felt utterly crushed at the time, believing that my grandmother deliberately was assuring Grampop's spending an eternity in perdition.

*Author's father and mother announce
wedding engagement, 1919*

*Author's father and mother on their
wedding day, June 16, 1920*

When my mother was a child she wanted desperately to become a teacher. Her father, however, decreed that girls do not need an education; so she quit school in the eighth grade, and worked as a telephone operator, earning three dollars and fifteen cents a week. Albert also quit school at the same time, and took a job in a secondhand store in Philadelphia. The job required him to use a pushcart, delivering heavy furniture every day throughout the city. The work was particularly onerous because Albert was undernourished, due partly because he had always been a finicky eater, and partly because his parents had little concern about his welfare.

Albert and author's mother on bikes 1915

Having his fill of this kind of labor, and reaching adulthood, Albert became a trolley car conductor. Because of his physical weakness he was unable to use the steel lever—a sort of crowbar—to throw the switches in the tracks; so he would have to ask a passenger, who was bigger and stronger than he, to do it for him. Wishing to supplement his income, he resorted to a bit of larceny. Rather than allowing the passengers to insert their coins in the deposit box that would ring when the fare was paid, he himself would take their coins and deposit them. That is to say, he would *presumably* deposit the coins in the box. He discovered that, when merely striking the box sharply with his hand, the bell denoting payment would ring without the coins actually entering the slot. Thus, he feigned inserting the coins, struck the box causing the bell to ring, and pocketed the money.

Uncle Bert (left) as trolley car conductor

It was ironic that Uncle Bert left this job to work for Willmark Service System, a security company, one of whose purposes was to detect dishonesty that might occur among a business establishment's employees. Willmark would send detectives, posing as "shoppers" to buy products or services, and report to the business owners any employees' misbehavior, such as ringing up false amounts on the cash register and pocketing the difference, or stealing merchandise for themselves. They also reported shoplifting, and provided advice for improving sales and merchandising techniques.

Uncle Bert went through the ranks as shopper, detective, and salesman, and finally became a vice president at the company's New York office. He established offices in major cities from coast to coast and in Canada, and would often be away from home for months at a time. On one occasion he lived in Seattle for two years, and in Chicago for a year, before returning home. Understandably, this kind of work was not conducive to having a wife and family. He was really a "loner," and his acquaintances either couldn't understand, or were amused by, his peculiar behavior at times.

He traveled to every state except Maine and California, meeting with corporation presidents and other business bigwigs, but he had hardly any social life. His only recreation was attending movie theaters almost every night; and he claimed to read the newspaper from cover to cover.

He feared more things than anyone else I have ever known. He was afraid to go swimming; he drove a car twenty miles an hour where the speed limit was forty; he refused to fly in an airplane; he was afraid to go to the top of the Statue of Liberty; and he denounced anyone who did any of these things. All kinds of things were either good or bad omens. He owned a nice wristwatch, and when he first wore it, he did not sell any contracts for Willmark. Wearing a watch was, for him, bad luck; so he gave the watch to me.

He always evaded questions that anyone might ask about his line of work. This was due undoubtedly to the secrecy involving detectives and clandestine shoppers in his company. When I was a young boy he told me that if anyone were to ask me what he did for a living, I was to say that he was an auditor. I didn't know what an auditor was, nor did I know until I was an adult the real nature of his occupation.

So secretive was he that he led his company's personnel to believe that he was divorced and had a son, "Artie." He was, of course, referring to me, his nephew. From the time I was a baby until becoming a teenager, I was the apple of Uncle Bert's eye. He always referred to me as "the Peanut," for reasons unknown; I was never small for my age.

He earned more money than anyone else in our family, and was a prime example of being one's proverbial "rich uncle." The presents I received from him at Christmas were always extravagant, costing more than my parents or any other friends or relatives were able or willing to buy for me. When I was a senior in high school he gave me a half carat diamond ring with

Author's Uncle Bert, c. 1933

Peanut inscribed on the inside of the solid gold band; and I wear it to this day.

Soon after Uncle Bert was earning good money with Willmark, he had the urge to learn to play the piano. He took a few lessons, and bought a small grand piano with the brand name, *Francis Bacon*. I was still using my mother's old upright piano, and it was in need of repair in addition to its periodic tuning. Since I anticipated making music my career, I wanted a better instrument. My piano teacher had two large grand pianos in her studio. One was a *Steinway* and the other was a German-made *Blüthner*. My teacher, as well as the music teacher in school, stated that a piano with good tone and sensitive key action was vital to developing my technique. When I told my father their opinions, he resented their input, and saw no reason to buy another piano.

Somehow or another, word about my being a potential candidate for a new piano came to the attention of a salesman in one of Philadelphia's department stores that sold the *Knabe* brand, a good, but not a top-of-the-line piano as was the *Steinway* or *Baldwin*. The *Knabe* salesman came to our home; and after I played a few pieces for him he declared—as might be expected—that I was a genius, and deserved a fine *Knabe* piano. At the time, a medium-sized *Knabe* grand cost six hundred dollars. When I approached my father about buying one, he said, "A piano won't take you anywhere. I can buy a car for that amount of money."

When Uncle Bert learned of my need for another piano, he offered to sell his *Francis Bacon* to my parents for one hundred dollars, since he never played it, constantly being away from home because of his job. His piano was in good condition, but was not the quality of instrument to which I was accustomed when taking my lessons. Nonetheless, it was an improvement over my mother's old one, and the price was acceptable. A piano mover asked three dollars to move Uncle Bert's piano from Grammom's house two doors away to our house, and to haul Mother's piano away for disposal. Rather than paying the moving fee, we gave Mother's piano and the piano stool to the mover in exchange for moving both instruments.

When Uncle Bert found out that I wanted to have some upgrading to his piano by way of tonal "voicing," key action adjustment, and tuning, he was insulted. He declared that *Francis Bacon* was the most superb piano in the world, and authorities told him that is was even better than a *Steinway*. It was useless to argue this matter with him. Subsequently, as years passed and I was earning my own living, I replaced his piano with a completely restored six-foot *Steinway* grand, and still later bought a brand new seven-foot *Steinway*—truly a magnificent instrument.

Uncle Bert wanted to "show off" his "son," Artie, to his business associates, and took me with him to visit the company's main office in New York City. It caused a terrible dilemma at which I shudder whenever I recall it. I was to be his "son," but he did not want to lie blatantly by introducing me as such. When I met one of his colleagues in the company,

Uncle Bert merely said to him, "I want you to meet Artie," but avoided identifying me as his son. He said beforehand that I was not to forget the ruse, so that I would not inadvertently refer to him as "Uncle," nor was I to call him "Dad."

The business executive to whom I was introduced invited us to dinner at his home in Scarsdale, an exclusive suburb of Manhattan. I had never before been in such posh surroundings. The house was a Mediterranean style mansion, having a sunken dining room, impressive chandeliers, oriental rugs, and almost every other feature that only the very wealthy could afford. The servants included a butler, a maid, a cook, and a gardener.

I had never been exposed to high society before, and other than being taught basic good manners, had no idea about which fork or spoon to use, or whether to cut the rolls, or tear them apart; and I didn't know that my napkin was to be unfolded and placed on my lap. While eating, I left the napkin folded and lying on the table, and the host said to me, "Artie, that's *your* napkin." Uncle Bert told me to unfold it and put it on my lap. I was thoroughly embarrassed during the entire meal!

Our host and his wife had a teenage son who played the piano. Because I had been a serious piano student for many years, Uncle Bert wanted to impress his host and his family by having me perform after dinner. After playing several pieces by Bach, Chopin, Mozart, and other recognized composers, I asked their son to play something, because his mother had spoken earlier about her son's inordinate talent for music. His mother, apparently not wishing to have revealed what must have been only mediocre musical ability, said something about its getting late, and he needed to go to bed. This was sort of a triumph for me, and I hoped that my bourgeois table manners during dinner might be overlooked.

Underlying this whole scenario was my fear of divulging unintentionally my real relationship as nephew rather than son. Suddenly the slipup occurred in the course of conversation when I addressed Bert as "Uncle." To this day, I can feel my face turning red with embarrassment and fright as I "let the cat out of the bag." I immediately endeavored to correct the situation and stammered something incoherent while trying to regain my composure; but strangely, my uncle ignored the situation, and our host did, too. This suggests that perhaps our host perceived Uncle Bert's deception at the onset, and he wished to avoid embarrassment.

Albert's being a fearful person played a role in his not being drafted into the military during World War II. He walked, rather than drove, four miles to the Camden armory where induction took place. My father suggested that Uncle Bert took the extra time to walk, rather than drive, in order to practice the role of being mentally, physically, and psychologically unable to serve in the army. He had often expressed to our immediate family his fear of going to war. His ploy worked; the examiners classified him as 4F for psychoneurosis.

When he came home after the examination he said that he didn't want anyone to know the real reason for being rejected, but preferred implying that he had a "social" disease. He told us, without going into detail, that the physical examination for venereal disease was loathsome and humiliating. This distressed me because I was almost eighteen years old, and knew that I would soon be going into the army. His hinting, without describing in detail his experience with the doctors, made me apprehensive about what awaited me when I would be going for induction.

Although he had more money than most people I knew, Uncle Bert was obsessively and inconsistently penurious in many respects. He was willing to own an expensive luxury automobile, but he followed procedures that defied rationality. His car had two heaters, which were designed to provide more than adequate comfort in cold weather; but he refused to turn them on because he believed they would run down the battery. To keep warm in winter, he and his mother would wrap themselves in blankets. He believed that the car had air conditioning, but it did not; and I told him so. When he would take his mother, my mother, and me in the car on a typical sweltering, summer day in New Jersey, he would insist that the windows remain closed, because one was not supposed to have open windows when the air conditioning was operating. We would be perspiring and in utter misery, but he would feign being comfortable in his "air conditioned" automobile.

On one occasion when I was with him in the

car at night, I noticed that he turned the headlights on and off while driving. He explained that headlights were not necessary when he drove in the vicinity of street lamps; so he would turn off the car lights when he was near the lamps, and turn them on after he had passed them.

In order to prevent putting stress on the car's engine, Uncle Bert would go miles out of the way to avoid using an overpass. He believed that the upslope of the road would wear out the engine prematurely. When approaching a traffic light or a stop street, he would remove his foot from the accelerator at least a half block from the intersection so that the brakes would require only a light tap, preventing the brake shoes from premature wear.

There were no garages at the row houses where he, his mother, and Grampop lived. Everybody in the neighborhood put his car in a rented garage located several blocks away. If Uncle Bert's car were parked by the curb in front of the house, and if it began to rain, he would rush out, drive to the garage to keep the car from getting wet, and walk several blocks home in the rain. He wanted to prevent the car from rusting.

After retiring at the age of fifty from Willmark, he stayed at home with his mother, looking after her every need. He took up the hobby of painting "by the numbers," a popular fad at the time whereby pre-drawn pictures had their segmented components numerically coded, indicating the paint color to be used. Needing diversion from remaining at home day and night, he would ask his mother whether he could to go out for an hour or so on Saturday night. She complained about being alone, but reluctantly agreed to let him go. He would take the bus or trolley car to Camden, which was about three miles distant, and stand on the corner at a busy intersection watching the people pass by. After an hour or so, he would stop at our house for a short visit, and then go home two doors away to his mother.

Despite his not behaving "like a man" in the traditional masculine sense, and having many quirks that seem to imply other than a macho image, he was not in the least bit effeminate in his gestures, gait, or speech. There were a number of occasions as a child, as well as an adult, when I was alone with him in hotels away from home, and there was not a scintilla of any indication that he was homosexual. He never referred to, nor was ever seen with, male friends. He was quite likely of the same sexual orientation as Isaac Newton, the mathematician, or George Frederick Handel, the composer. Neither ever had, or needed, female companionship.

When I was a toddler, Uncle Bert promised my mother that he would pay my way to attend Princeton University. He thought this was a good choice of schools because the dining halls were reportedly furnished with sterling silver tableware and linen napkins. Being a person of financial means, and doting on me as he did, my mother and I believed that he could, indeed, live up to this promise. When I was about to graduate from high school, and having successfully passed college entrance examinations, any mention of my going to Princeton quickly subsided. Uncle Bert propounded a new outlook for me by stating that college was a waste of time, and that he, a self-made man, never went to college, and look how successful he was! He reneged on sending me to Princeton, so I went on a scholarship to Temple University, majoring in music.

I was enthusiastic about my studies, and related to my parents and my uncle the kinds of things I was learning. Uncle Bert reacted by saying that college professors are stupid, and that those who went to college were "a bunch of punks." He declared that he knew more than any of the professors. He bragged about doing things the hard way, and claimed that he did not need an academic education to walk the city streets, selling contracts for Willmark. When he denigrated college students and professors, I made the mistake of telling him that I expected to make my living with my head instead of my feet. This may have been the straw that broke the proverbial camel's back. Virtually from that time on, there was always an aura of antagonism that tainted our relationship.

The rancor was reduced somewhat when I went into military service shortly after my eighteenth birthday and after a semester of college. Quite possibly, Uncle Bert's dodging the draft tweaked his conscience a bit, and he was devastated by the thought of my going to war in his stead, so to speak. I remember vividly saying goodbye to him as I was leaving for camp. He hugged me tightly and sobbed uncontrollably. My parents were also unhappy about my going to war, and their seeing Uncle Bert bawl so pitiably did nothing towards consoling them on my departure.

Chapter 3

"Cousin" Robert

I had other uncles, too; but their lives and attitudes were not as bizarre as Uncle Bert's. My father's brother, Alfred, died at the age of twenty-six; I was six years old. He became, in a way, a part of my mother's family by marrying Grampop's granddaughter, Mildred. The marriage was stormy, and Alf came to live with my parents and me. They had no children, and Uncle Alf admitted that I was his favorite nephew. His said that his other nephew and niece always had runny noses, and when he was around them at mealtimes, he became nauseated.

There was an incident when he was a dental patient sitting in the dentist chair. In order to hold Alf's jaws apart, the dentist applied a clamp-like device with a screw adjustment. The dentist was talking with his assistant, and not paying attention to how wide Alf's mouth was being pried open. Alf pointed to his mouth, trying to communicate that it was uncomfortable. The dentist, engaged in conversation with the nurse, and not heeding Alf's complaint, continued turning the adjustment screw until the corners of Alf's mouth were tearing. When there was no response to Alf's complaint, Alf punched the dentist, sending him into the nurse, and both of them flew out a nearby window. Luckily, the office was on the first floor, and the two suffered only minor injuries.

He had no for-mal education higher than grade school, and found it difficult to find satisfactory employ-ment. My father was able to procure a job for him as a machin-ist apprentice at Arm-strong Cork Company in Camden, where my father was superinten-dent of maintenance. Uncle Alf had hardly worked there a few weeks before he was electrocuted in the factory. He was attempting to repair a brass light socket hanging from the ceiling. It was a hot summer day, and he was perspiring and leaning on a machine of some sort. The socket was not insulated, and Uncle Alf's body carried the cur-rent fatally from power source to ground.

Author's father at Armstrong Cork Company

Author's father, paternal grandmother
Della Birkby, and Uncle Alf, c. 1918

Shortly before Alf died, he and his wife Mildred, and her brother and his wife were in a terrible automobile accident about sixty miles from home. They telephoned my father, and he made the two-hour drive to the scene of the crash. When he arrived at the site, there were still no police or ambulance present, and my father took the injured back to their home. Mildred's brother was the driver, and was thrown against the steering wheel, fracturing several ribs. Alf's face struck the windshield, and his lower teeth pierced his lower lip so that when he took a drink of water, it leaked through the punctures. Mildred suffered two broken legs and internal injuries, making her bed-ridden for weeks. She was still confined to bed when Alf was electrocuted.

It is a spooky coincidence that my parents and I were in an accident on the same road, route 30, the

Lincoln Highway, only a short distance from the crash involving Mildred and Alf. We were on our way to Washington, Pennsylvania, as was our custom every summer, to visit my father's mother, sisters, and their families. A car came from a side road without stopping for the intersection, and smashed into the side of our car. Few cars had trunks in that era, and our suitcases were carried on the running board, held in place by a metal luggage carrier resembling an expandable gate used to confine pets or children within a room. All of the baggage was torn from the running board, and its contents strewn on the highway.

No one was injured, but there was considerable damage to both vehicles. An Italian woman in the other car, whose husband was driving, said to him, "You're drunk, you fool! I told you that you shouldn't be driving!" Had there been police on the scene, we would have had legal recourse for payment of damages; but nothing came of it.

In the weeks following Alf's funeral, my father, mother, and I would go to Camden to visit Mildred to assist her as she was recuperating from her severe injuries, and to console her for the loss of her husband. Mildred lived with her parents, "Uncle" Rob and "Aunt" Ella. Rob was one of Grampop's sons who operated a makeshift cigar store in his home. Also living in the household were Mildred's nephew and niece, Robert and Mildred.

I was six years old at the time, and Robert was about ten. I had no brothers or sisters of my own; and with my father having engaged in hardly any activities with me, Robert was someone to whom I could look for fun and information. His father, who drove the car in which Mildred and Alf were injured, was divorced, and he and his wife had hardly any contact with their children. Hence, his kids lived with their grandparents, Rob and Ella, and their Aunt Mildred.

It would serve little purpose to go into detail about this family tree; but it is necessary merely to mention that my family was related through two bloodlines by marriage to Robert, whereby I thought of him as my cousin, and regarded him as a close friend. I could write a book containing our many adventures and activities, but shall mention only a few.

Cousin Robert, his sister Mildred, my "real" cousin Alberta and her parents, and I with my parents, were on a picnic at a park in south Jersey. After eating lunch we four children went for a hike in the woods adjoining the park. It was a completely undeveloped jungle-like area with no roads, and only sporadic, unmarked footpaths. After roaming about aimlessly, we became hopelessly lost. The girls and I were frightened, doubting that we would ever be found. Robert, the oldest of our group, maintained his composure, assuring us that he would return us to safety. Whenever we came to a fork or an intersection in the path, he spit into the palm of his hand, tapped the saliva with the forefinger of his other hand, and noted the direction in which it squirted. We took the path that most closely matched the heading of the squirt. We were lost for several hours, and did not find our way back to the picnic. We arrived at a promontory overlooking a lake, and just sat there, realizing that Robert's pseudo-scientific direction finder was flawed. Understandably, our families were panic-stricken, and my father and Uncle Alphonse went looking for us. We were finally found, but upon hearing that we youngsters were perched high above a lake in a precarious location, my mother scolded us severely. From that time onward, she did not trust Robert's sense of judgment or responsibility, and made certain that I was within hailing distance when we visited him.

Robert showed me a lot of unique things to which I had never before been exposed. He showed me how he could put me to sleep in a few moments, and I learned subsequently that the procedure is extremely dangerous, and can be fatal. He stood behind me with his arms around my chest, and with his hands grasping each other. He squeezed tightly, and told me to take three deep, slow breaths. I was ordered to hold the third breath for several seconds, and then exhale. At that point, he relaxed his grasp, and I fell unconscious to the floor. Sad to relate, I performed this "sleep-inducing" procedure on a number of my schoolmates, not realizing the risks. Fortunately, none of my "patients" were harmed, and after learning of its potential hazard, I never did it again.

During this time—I was not yet a teenager—I was fascinated by firearms, but didn't know the difference between bullets, shells, cartridges, or any other such terminology. Robert had two cap pistols, and handed me one of them to shoot. We inserted the caps, but he said—without actually showing me close-up—that my gun was loaded with toy caps, but that his gun was loaded with blanks. He said—and I believed him—that blanks were missiles just like bullets, and were capable of making holes in anything they struck. There was an old dilapidated cinder block garage at the end of his back yard, and he said that both of us should shoot at it. We fired several shots, and we went to see the results of our shooting. I saw no damage from my caps, but Robert directed my attention to some unevenly shaped small holes in the mortar between the cinder blocks. These, he declared, were the result of the blanks that came from his gun. I was genuinely impressed, and wanted to see the actual ammunition that he purportedly loaded into his pistol. He evaded my request with some elusive explanation about the jeopardy of exposing an underage child to the mysterious ammunition. He was a young con artist in a manner of speaking, but no harm was done.

There were a couple of Robert's entertaining gimmicks that I showed to my own son many years later. They are safe when done cautiously by a responsible adult, but Robert's doing them with me while we were without supervision created a real atmosphere of excitement. One trick employed six flat toothpicks placed on a flat surface, three in one direction and three on top of them at ninety degrees. They were slightly bent so that, when they were interlaced above and below each other, they formed a stressed lattice where the toothpicks crossed. When a lit match was applied to a corner where the toothpicks were joined, the flame would destroy the joint, and the picks, being under tension, would fly delightfully in all directions.

Another experiment also required fire, the phenomenon that has intrigued children for eons. A straight pin was placed on a flat book match along its length so that the point of the pin touched the head of the match. Next, a small sheet of tinfoil was wrapped tightly around the head of the match, the pin, and the entire length of the match stem. Then the pin was removed, forming a hollow space between the head of the match and the other end. The match was set on a narrow support so that the front and back of the "rocket" were not touching anything. Then a lit match was held so that the flame touched the foil-wrapped head. The heat ignited the enclosed head, and its jet of gas was forced out the back, causing the rocket to fly perhaps twenty feet away. We were making our own fireworks on a small scale!

Robert's father had a private pilot's license in the 1920's, a rarity in those times. Robert set up a simulated cockpit using a yardstick for the joystick, two mousetraps on the floor representing rudder pedals, and a clothespin for the throttle. He showed me how an airplane took off by using full throttle, with joystick forward until rotation speed was reached, and then pulling back on the stick. The rudder pedals were moved to counteract engine torque.

Flying became Robert's passion, and he became a bomber pilot in World War II. His plane was shot down on a bombing run over Europe, and he was never heard from. One of his friends in another plane on the same mission subsequently contacted Robert's family, saying that he saw the aircraft go down, and crewmen bailing out, but had no way of knowing whether Robert was among them.

In addition to periodic visits, I was always certain to see "Cousin" Robert and his sister at New Years Eve parties. These were the biggest get-togethers for relatives by blood and marriage on both sides of my family. Always present were my father, mother, Grampop, Grammom, Uncle Alphonse and Aunt Bertha, their daughter (cousin Alberta), Robert's grandparents (Rob and Ella), and their daughter, Mildred (Alf's widow).

Each family would take its turn in hosting the party, and tradition assured that the food would always be the same. It was referred to as a "Dutch" lunch, "Dutch" being a corrupted form of "deutsch," meaning "German." It consisted of pumpernickel bread, Limburger cheese, boiled ham, baked ham, Schweitzer cheese, potato salad, Kosher dill pickles, either pickled or smoked herring, beer, and wine. These items were always purchased early in the evening of the party at a Jewish delicatessen named Ostrov's in Fairview, a suburb of Camden. The men from each family did the buying and split the cost among them. There were few concerns in those days about gout, heart attack, diabetes, or obesity, and everyone ate as though there were no tomorrow.

At the stroke of midnight all of the men gave silver coins from their pocket change to the women who were present, and everyone was required for good luck to eat a piece of herring. The young children, myself included, hated this regimen, and resisted eating what we regarded as being horrible tasting and unfit for human consumption, but we were compelled to do so, lest we suffer misfortune in the coming year. (I no longer have these sentiments about herring; I relish it now!)

It was also necessary for insuring good luck for the ensuing year that the first person to enter the home must be a man having dark skin. All of the family members were of English or German background, and no one was really swarthy. Uncle Alphonse, my mother's brother, was somewhat darker than anyone else; so he would have to leave the house from the back door, and then come to the front door, ring the doorbell, and be invited to enter. Everyone would gasp in mock surprise that we had the great fortune to have a dark man be the first person to visit in the New Year. I asked my mother why these practices would assure us of a bright future, and her response was simply that they were time-honored, and "they" say that bad luck will be the result of breaking this tradition.

We kids always had noisemakers of one sort or another—toy horns, pots and pans, or whatever—and on a few occasions the men would go outside and shoot a few bullets from my father's .32-caliber revolver. I was not permitted to be with them when the gun was fired, but I thought that to be the ultimate macho means of celebrating New Year's Eve.

I had less fun playing with my "real" cousin Alberta than with Robert, because she was a girl. However, I enjoyed several vacations with her and her parents when they accompanied me and my parents for a weekend in Atlantic City. The six of us stayed in one room of a three-story, seedy hotel off the boardwalk. It may have cost a total of ten dollars for two nights' lodging. There were two double beds, one for my parents and one for Uncle Al and Aunt Bertha, and Cousin Alberta and I slept on cots.

The sign on the front of the building advertised "running water." Dad suggested that it might refer to holes in the roof. The rug was old and worn with fringes on the edges. Again, making light of the less-than-elegant accommodations, Dad described the rug as having appliqué. A red "fire exit" light in the hall shined through the transom over our bedroom door. Aunt Bertha happened to bring an umbrella on the trip, and hung it, opened, across the transom window to keep the room dark during the night. Uncle Al was always the jokester in the family, and regaled us with nonsensical fun until the wee hours.

Dad had a corn on his toe to which he applied Fireman's and Policeman's Salve, an ointment designed to burn off the corn. Everyone was in a mirthful mood, and laughed hilariously when he declared that the salve took off his toe, but the corn remained.

Everybody finally fell asleep, but at about four o'clock in the morning a truck on the street below our open window crashed into a scavenger's push-cart, sending its contents clattering to the ground. No one seemed to be injured, and this mild excitement was regarded merely as another humorous episode to be enjoyed.

We did what everyone else did in Atlantic City in those days: we bathed in the ocean, sat on the beach, visited Steel Pier and Hamid's Pier, walked on the boardwalk, ate frozen custard cones and salt water taffy, watched artists on the beach next to the boardwalk draw impromptu portraits, observed auctions in boardwalk salesrooms, and watched people pass by.

Dad and Uncle Al shared expenses, and while dividing costs, discovered that four dollars was unaccounted for, and each was unwilling to take the money. They came up with the idea of buying toy banks from a souvenir shop for Alberta and me, and putting two dollars in each of them. They gave them to us as we were sitting in a boardwalk pavilion amongst other vacationers, and said nothing to anybody about the money they had put in the banks.

The banks were metal, and made in the likeness of little buckets with a slot in the top and a locked door in the bottom. Alberta and I eagerly inserted the keys in our banks to see how they worked, and—lo and behold—each bank contained two dollars in bills! In those days, two dollars was the equivalent of a couple of weeks' allowance, and discovering this treasure was unimaginable. Watching us find this unexpected treasure were several parents with their children. Not realizing that our banks containing money was a "put-up" job, they asked where we bought the banks, and gave their kids money to buy all that were in stock.

Early one morning Dad and Uncle Al left the two ladies, Alberta, and me in the room, and went to a corner store to by a couple of cigars. When they returned, Al in his constant state of doing anything for a laugh, banged on the door and yelled, "Huckster!" Our room was on the third floor, but Al was at the door of a look-alike room on the second floor. Dad glanced at the number on the door and told Al they were at the wrong room. Both men ran down the hall and up the stairs before the rudely awakened guests saw who was at their door.

Atlantic City weekend. Top row, left to right: Aunt Bertha, author's mother, and author's father. Bottom row: cousin Alberta, author, and Uncle Al.

Another case of mistaken room identity happened when my father took Mother in the car to pick me up after my piano lesson. Hilda Radey, my teacher, had her studio on the second floor of an apartment on Haddon Avenue in Collingswood. Mother told Dad to go upstairs and go right into the studio; it wasn't necessary to knock.

He followed her instructions, but they were at an identical-looking building a block away. Dad walked in, and rather than entering the music studio, met two young women in lingerie in their bedroom. They shrieked and grabbed a blanket to cover themselves. My father dashed out of the room, down the steps, and to the car, and told my mother that her oversight almost got him arrested.

Chapter 4
Hub and Dad

Earnest was one of my father's brothers, and worked as a laborer in the construction business. For reasons that no one seemed to know, he was addressed as Uncle "Hub." While walking on the girders of a building being erected, Uncle Hub was knocked from the fifth story by a crane that was rotating from one position to another. As he was falling towards the ground, he reached out with one arm and, as he was passing the hook of the crane, grabbed the hook, and dangled several stories over the street below. The crane operator, seeing him hanging there, hollered, "Hey! What are you doing there?" Uncle Hub let out an expletive and told him to take him down.

While working on another building, Uncle Hub lost his balance and fell down several stories in an elevator shaft. At the bottom was a container of wet concrete into which he plummeted, and sustained no injuries.

Hub led a dissolute life and was in jail a number of times for various crimes, and my father was always paying his bail. In one instance when Hub came home drunk, he had an argument with his mother, and slapped her. My father was present, and he punched Hub in the jaw, knocking him unconscious. Hub fell, and his head became jammed between the kitchen stove and the wall. My father notified Hub that, were he ever to strike his mother again, my father would kill him.

After my father had just purchased a new suit and overcoat, Hub was going on a date with his girl-friend and borrowed my father's new apparel. Hub's girlfriend lived out of town and he didn't have a car, so he walked to the highway, intending to hitchhike to her house. He was picked up by a couple of bad guys who beat him, stole his money, and threw him out of the car while it was moving at high speed. He landed on the side of the road, and his face smashed into a mound of mud-like clay. A passing automobile espied him lying motionless, and took him back to town where he was recognized, and then taken to his house. My father related to me how he used a tea-spoon to dig out the soil that was packed solidly in his brother's mouth.

Hub's girlfriend worked behind the bar at a saloon owned by the girl's father. Her father didn't approve of Hub (which was understandable), and told his daughter that she was to have nothing to do with him. One day Hub entered the saloon to pick up his girl for a date. Her father was there, and told Hub to leave. He refused to do so, and when the police were called, Hub picked up some bottles on the bar and threw them into the large mirrors behind the counter, smashing them into smithereens. Before the police arrived, Hub reached over the counter, picked up his girlfriend bodily and carried her out to his car.

As he drove away, he came to an intersection where traffic was controlled by a cop standing in the street, operating a mechanical stop-and-go signal, which was a forerunner of the electric traffic light. Hub went through the stop signal and drove over the cop's feet. Hub kept going, but waved back at the cop and shouted, "Hi, Buddy!"

Hub moved to Youngstown, Ohio, and wanted to visit his mother, brothers and sisters in Washington, Pennsylvania where, incidentally, my father was born. He no longer owned a car, and he didn't have money for train fare. The commonplace solution in that era to accessing inexpensive travel was riding freight trains. When there was no room in a freight car, or if the doors were locked, hobos "rode the rods" underneath the cars. This was the option used by Hub. It was winter, and bitterly cold. While lying under the freight car, his coat was dangling and coming in contact with the ground and the railroad ties. Fearful that the coat might become entangled with a switch or other protuberance, Hub removed his coat, dropping it between the tracks, and went the rest of the way wearing only his shirt and trousers. How he survived without freezing to death, or at least suffering frostbite, was a miracle. After all of his harrowing episodes, he died of a heart attack in his forties, while leaning over to lift a wheelbarrow at a construction job.

Unlike his brother, my father was never in trouble with the law; but as a kid he was a prankster, and was not a good example for me to follow. He told me about smearing Limburger cheese on the smoke-stack of the pot-bellied stove in the schoolroom. When the teacher started the fire, the heated smoke-stack brought out the stench of the cheese, driving everyone out of the building.

During a music class, the teacher gave the pupils a written test on the rudiments of music nota-tion. She told the kids that when they were finished the test they could go home. Dad wrote his name on the paper and, as far as he was concerned, he was fin-ished; so he went home. Merely for writing his name and turning in an otherwise blank sheet of paper, Dad received a grade of twenty percent!

Most kids played marbles in those days, and my father filled his pants pockets to bulging with dozens of them. In the midst of quiet time when everyone was told to study, Dad turned his pockets inside out, allowing all of the marbles to clatter noisily on the floor.

I was never a skilled marble player, and mar-veled that Dad was able to accumulate enough to fill his pockets. He showed me how to acquire a large collection without being an expert at playing the game. We used a small, empty pasteboard carton that had contained birdseed. This type of box had a hole in the top about an inch in diameter that contained a metal cap insert. We removed the cap and were "in business."

I would ask a marble-playing friend to stand up and hold a marble at arm's length over the hole in the box. Then I directed him to attempt to drop the marble into the hole. For every marble that went into the hole, I would give back three marbles of my own. To execute this maneuver is not as easy as it sounds, but it appeared to be an easy challenge by my friends who tried it. As expected (by me, not my friends), only rarely would the patsy's marble enter the hole; and I would readily reward him with three marbles. The marbles that missed the hole and fell outside the box were mine to keep, and the marbles that went into the box were also mine. Somehow or another, my friends who lost their marbles, attributed it to their own ineptitude in dropping them accurately into the hole, and did not see that they were at a disadvantage. In no time at all, I had an enviable collection of beautiful marbles of every sort.

Dad's father died of a heart attack, and as the oldest boy, Dad quit school in the fourth grade to support the family. There were nine children in the family and nine dollars on which to live. His mother did laundry and took in boarders to help make ends meet. My father lived on a farm in the summer. After harvest time he moved back into town and worked three jobs. He had a paper route in the wee hours, and worked full shifts in a glass factory that made Mason jars, and in a steel mill.

An acquaintance made Dad aware that these jobs offered no future, and recommended that he learn a trade. He carefully considered various options that were described to him, and chose to become an apprentice machinist. He worked four years to become a journeyman machinist at Tyler Tube and

Pipe Company.

To foster good will among the employees, and between them and management, the company sponsored a series of athletic competitions. Dad was of medium build, but was agile and muscular. He entered all of the track and field games, and was awarded a large, solid gold medal for being the all-round champion, winning first place in all events. He wore the medal on his watch chain across his vest, and I still cherish it to this day as a memento.

One of the competitors challenged the out-come of one of the races, contending that he had won rather than my father. This was not particularly unusual, because there were no electronic timers in those days, which could determine a winner with certainty. Despite this participant's assertion that he was the winner, the judges awarded the victory to Dad. This challenge of the results piqued my father, and he offered to run the race again. On the re-running, Dad won by several lengths, assuring his rightful claim as winner. His adversary, humiliated, left the company.

When it seemed that America would become embroiled in the First World War, and the military draft was inevitable, my father sought employment that might prevent him from being called. While Tyler Tube's manufacturing vital war material could potentially offer military deferment, Dad surmised that working in wartime industry, and moving to another location, would increase the likelihood of escaping military service. To achieve this end, he moved from Washington, Pennsylvania to Camden, New Jersey, home of New York Shipyard, where he worked as a machinist, installing propeller shafts in naval vessels. At war's end, shipbuilding dwindled, and Dad went to work for Armstrong Cork Company, mentioned earlier.

Chapter 5
Unrivaled Thrift

I related earlier Uncle Bert's living with his mother, and being utterly devoted to her every need. Not wanting to entrust her care to anyone else, Bert retired in his fifties so that he could be with her constantly. He could afford to have a live-in companion take care of her and do the housework, but he chose to assume that role himself. He did all of the cooking, cleaning, washing and ironing; and when the day's chores were finished, he and his mother would sit in the front yard and watch the traffic on Haddon Avenue go by.

Grammom's hearing was deteriorating, and she could no longer converse easily, use the telephone, or listen to the radio. Her friends and my parents suggested that it was time for her to be fitted with a hearing aid. The idea appealed to Grammom, but Albert convinced her that there was a danger of being electrocuted by the batteries, and that the acid from the batteries would spill, burning her skin and ruining her clothing. After she was sold this "bill of goods," she believed her son, feeling that he was genuinely looking after her best interest. Albert's reluctance to spend money has already been alluded to in the treatment of his automobile.

Grammom's eyesight also went bad, and it was

not long before she was completely blind. As time went on, she incurred more and more debilitation from old age, but she hardly ever went to a doctor. On the one or two rare instances of her having a doctor's treatment, Albert would throw the medication down the toilet, saying that doctors knew nothing, and were trying to kill his mother.

The reluctance to seek medical help was a family trait. At the age of thirteen, I complained of pain in my abdomen. My mother and father did not call a doctor, believing that my "tummy ache" would soon go away. My mother gave me an enema, but my condition got worse. Finally a doctor was called, and stated that I had appendicitis. My mother felt really bad when the doctor told her that an enema was the worst thing she could have done. It was feared that the appendix had burst, and that peritonitis may have set in.

The decision was made to take me to the hospital, and my father tried to assuage my apprehension by telling me that I would merely have ice packs applied, rather than undergoing surgery. The ambulance arrived, and I was carried down the stairs and out of the house, sitting on a chair, which was carried by my father and the neighbor next door. It never occurred to us to ask why no stretcher was available. My grandmother came over to see me being taken away and wailed, "Ach, Gott! Ach Gott! This is the end!" She always believed that going to a hospital was a sure indication that death was near; they were places in which to die.

The appendectomy was a success, and the surgeon said that my appendix was inflamed and on the verge of bursting. My parents believed that there was no such crisis, and that the doctor had to offer that explanation to "save face." My mother complained that I should not have been such a sissy by admitting to pain when the doctor pressed on my abdomen during diagnosis. I know that she loved me dearly; but she said that I would not have required hospitalization had I been more stoical.

After a few days in the hospital, I was afflicted with pleural pneumonia. I woke up one night with such severe chest pain that I could not take a breath. The nurses and an intern came into the room, but did not know what to do. Finally they called the hospital chief of staff, Dr. Wesley Jack, and he directed them to wrap strips of tape tightly around my chest and back as a temporary measure to restrict my chest expansion while breathing. It was explained that the pleura was the membrane that lined the chest cavity and covered the lungs, and reducing movement would lessen friction between pleura, lungs, and chest wall.

The next day a device was brought into the room to treat the pleurisy more effectively. It contained a long coil of rubber-insulated electric cable that was wound around my chest, providing heat that would presumably eliminate my discomfort. In those days, hospital charges were presented each day as treatments were administered. The bill for the electric cable machine was about fifteen dollars or so, and

I felt guilty after my mother complained about the expense. What made her particularly angry at having to pay this bill was her noticing a sheaf of papers that the nurse inadvertently left on my hospital bureau. It listed names of patients and showed how much each had to pay for treatment. Apparently some were welfare patients, or "on relief," as was the description of those who were indigent. There were a number of people with the designation of "no charge" after their names, and my mother complained that she was paying other people's medical expenses.

She never learned to drive a car, so she had to take the bus or trolley car to visit me in the hospital. Again, I felt guilty because she told me how tired she was after doing what were to her important and necessary daily tasks, such as washing, ironing, sewing, baking, and cleaning, and then taking time to come to Camden where the hospital was located.

My father could not take her because he worked during the day for the cork company, and worked every night after supper until midnight at his own machine shop. He rented a barn several blocks from home and equipped it with two metal lathes, two drill presses, a shaper, a power hack saw, and a couple of grinders. All of the large machines were operated by belts and pulleys suspended from the ceiling, and powered by a three horsepower, three phase motor. It was typical in those days to have one motor and a line shaft for several machines, whereas in modern factories, each machine has its own electric motor. The system that my father installed was recognized as being hazardous when changing the speed at which a machine was operating. It required the machinist to slide his hand under the moving drive belt to transfer it to varying sized pulleys. In those days protective guards around spinning gears, belts, and blades were rarely used. State inspectors visited periodically and required guards to be installed; but as soon as the inspector would leave, the guards would be removed. Workers thought the protective shields to be a nuisance.

I enjoyed watching Dad using the shop equipment, but he discouraged me from being there because of the ever-present danger in a machine shop's environment. I never cease to marvel how my father moved and installed all of this heavy equipment virtually by himself. The shear physical labor of fastening the large, five-hundred pound motor and the overhead drive shaft and pulley system is daunting!

Dad learned about an auction in New Brunswick, New Jersey, at which a factory that was going out of business was selling its entire machine shop. He wanted to buy a couple of machines at a bargain price. Paul Scholz, a neighbor across the street, owned a print block business that manufactured rollers for printing wallpaper; and hearing that Dad was going to the auction, asked to go along, hoping also to buy some equipment for his establishment. Mother and I, and Mrs. Scholz went along for the ride.

The machine shop was huge, and contained many items that were on Dad's "wish list." While waiting for the auction to begin, Dad and Mr. Scholz saw several small items that they wanted. These included, among other things, several "dogs" used for setting up a lathe operation, a lathe chuck and a lathe faceplate twenty-two inches in diameter. These pieces were worth several hundred dollars; but rather than bidding on them, they tossed them from a factory window, went outside to retrieve them, and took them to the car. When they went back into the factory, it was announced that no individual machines would be sold. Rather, the entire factory's equipment would be up for auction. This was in 1936 when Dad's new Dodge automobile cost $910, and he gave my mother $10 per week to pay for all the food and my piano lesson. The purchase of the factory, lock, stock, and barrel, was beyond the reach of most individuals. We watched the auction, and within a minute's time everything was auctioned to a business conglomerate from New York for $10,000. Dad had no qualms about acquiring the items without paying for them.

I was with him and Mother at the Farmers Market near the Delaware Bridge in Camden. As we walked from one produce truck to another, buying various items, I said to Dad, "Where did you get that flashlight?" It was lit, and protruding from his hip pocket.

He hissed, "Shut up!" Mother uttered a subdued chastisement for his dishonesty, but was afraid to make an issue of it. He had many tools in his basement, but bought hardly any of them. Dad's crimes were not as obvious or—who's to say—as egregious as those of his brother, but he was never caught or imprisoned.

My mother's brother, Alphonse, whose first occupation was barbering, learned the machinist trade, and owned a machine shop in Camden. It was a very successful enterprise, and his specialty was manufacturing and repairing small, highly specialized items such as underwater cameras and medical equipment. In contrast, my father worked with large items in commercial laundries, paper mills, breweries, and bronze foundries. Dad's primary employer, Armstrong Cork Company, frowned upon "moonlighting," or working two jobs, but he continued doing so openly for many years, and his boss never realized it.

Chapter 6

"Uncle" Sylvester

Among our friends were Sylvester and Edith, who lived down the street about a half block away. They first became acquainted with us when Edith and my mother worked together as operators in the telephone company. Before Sylvester married Edith, he owned a fleet of barges, and made a lot of money hauling freight on the Delaware River. When they married, Edith no longer had to work, and they went to Cuba for their honeymoon. He sold his company for a handsome profit, and retired at age thirty-five.

Not content with a life of idle luxury, Sylvester bought several orchards near Pitman, New Jersey, and raised peaches and apples. The conditions for growing fruit in southern Jersey were ideal, and Sylvester prospered in his new occupation. He worked like a madman, doing all the labor by himself. He planted, pruned, and sprayed the trees, harvested the fruit, and carried it in his truck to market in Camden and Philadelphia.

He purchased adjoining land and needed to clear it of natural growth trees to make room for expanding his orchards. He asked my father to design and build a machine that could pull stumps from the ground after the trees were cut down. Within a very short time, Dad constructed a motorized stump puller that utilized steel cables that wrapped around the tree roots and removed them completely from the ground. The device worked as desired, but shortly after putting it to the task, Sylvester got his hand caught between the cables and cut his finger so that it was hanging by a thread.

I was at home when Sylvester stopped by to tell Dad about the accident, and remember seeing his hand wrapped in a piece of black, dirty cloth. When he went to the doctor, he was told that the finger could possibly be re-attached; but Sylvester said to cut it off.

Sylvester raised a number of varieties of peaches, including Hale, Elberta, and Redbirds. One of the obnoxious and time-consuming elements of being a fruit grower was sorting it into various sizes. Up until that time there was no automated method of accomplishing this chore; so again, Sylvester asked my father whether he could invent a means of separating peaches into small, medium, and large sizes without bruising them. Dad drew up some original specifications and said he could make a machine to do the job, and it would cost three hundred dollars.

Sylvester agreed to the terms, but shortly afterward wanted to change the sorter's capability by increasing its capacity and speed of operation. Amid the construction, Dad changed its design to accommodate the new requirements, and this necessitated different materials and altered mechanical features. When Dad explained that the alterations would cost more, Sylvester readily agreed, and was pleased with what seemed to be a bargain.

The new grader was delivered and worked "like a charm," but Sylvester had second thoughts about paying the increased amount. He flatly refused to pay anything at all, and complained that the fruit was being destroyed as it went through the grading process. Dad sued for the full cost of building the machine, and won the case. Sylvester ignored the court order to pay, and the two men avoided each other. Edith had nothing to do with the matter, and we maintained our amicable relationship with her. She told us that her husband could be unreasonable, and regretted his callous behavior.

Perhaps as long as five years later, Sylvester came to our house, and as he rang the doorbell, saw my father sitting by the window in the living room. Sylvester looked in the window, smiled and waved, but my father just sat there, ignoring him. Mother went to the door and let him in. Sylvester acknowledged that what he did was wrong, and peeled off five one hundred dollar bills to cover the cost of the improved peach grader.

My father was typically an absolutely non-forgiving man, and would hold a grudge forever. I was surprised and pleased that Dad was willing to let the matter rest. It was no time at all until the relationship was completely healed, and continued for many years.

"Aunt" Eef and "Uncle" Sylvester, c. 1938

My parents vacationed at their cottage atop Mount Hebron in North Carolina a number of times, and visited their home in Fort Lauderdale for extended periods. After I grew up and married, my wife, son, and I also took vacations at their places.

Their Florida home was on an inland waterway, and Sylvester owned a 24-foot cabin cruiser that was moored at his own dock. He and Edith, and my wife and I once went out in his boat for a short cruise. The craft did not have a very deep keel, and it was virtually impossible to hold it on course. No matter what speed we went, the boat would veer from one side of the channel to the other; the slightest movement of the helm overcompensated, causing us to bump into the shoreline.

There were numerous drawbridges on the waterway, and one is supposed to blow the boat's horn when approaching to signal the drawbridge operator. The clutch on Sylvester's boat was defective, and we could not stop the boat while waiting for the bridge to be raised. The only recourse was to stop the engine, and this caused the boat to drift uncontrolled into the bank. At each drawbridge, the engine had to be restarted, and we would reverse to back away from the bank before proceeding under the bridge.

We finally left the waterway and were out in the ocean in the shipping lane. Our ship-to-shore radio was inoperable—Sylvester didn't see any need for it—and we had no means of communicating with anyone. Suddenly we were in the midst of large ocean-going vessels bearing down on us and blowing their horns. I told Sylvester that this was no place for us, and that we should return to a waterway and head for home.

During the whole afternoon's outing, in addition to the clutch's not working, and our inability to hold a straight course, the engine was running roughly, suggesting fouled plugs or need for a tune-up. Not surprisingly, as we tried to get out of the way of the ships, our engine stalled. Sylvester opened the engine hatch and tried to do whatever had to be done to get us going again; and meanwhile, we were drifting out of control, hoping to avoid colliding with another vessel. Whatever corrective measure Sylvester resorted to, he managed to restart the engine, enabling us to limp back to his dock. What should have been a fun-filled experience turned out to be a nightmare!

Chapter 7
Closet Skeletons

I t's ironic that Sylvester, who was the only personal friend for whom my father did any work in his machine shop, was the only one whose unwillingness to pay for services resulted in a lawsuit. When Dad retired from Armstrong, he also gave up his own shop. Business establishments for whom he had worked, however, called upon him regularly as a consultant. This mild semi-retirement kept him active and helped pay the bills.

Life for my parents was pleasant and uncomplicated until Grammom died. In her final days, Albert was a wreck, unable to cope with the thought of her leaving him. He asserted, in all earnestness, that he would not let her die. When she did, he was inconsolable, and remained so until his own death at the age of seventy.

After Grammom's departure, Albert moved in with my mother and father, and occupied an upstairs bedroom. He was afraid of ghosts, and feared that the spirit of his mother—or any other deceased person—would return to haunt him. To prevent this from happening, he placed a chair at the head of the stairs to block any phantasm from encroaching.

He felt isolated upstairs, and was worried about escaping if a fire were to occur. His solution to this concern was to tie a long coil of rope to the hot water radiator by the window, so he would have a means of climbing down to the outside if necessary. The notion of his lowering himself on a rope from an upper story to the ground was beyond anyone's wildest imagination.

He suspected that passers-by out on the street, or those looking from their windows at my parents' house, were trying to spy on him. He wanted to prevent anyone from detecting any pattern to his regimen or behavior, so he would turn on and off the light in his room periodically during the day and night in order that no one would know exactly when he went to bed. To confuse the would-be nosey-pokers even more effectively, he raised and lowered the window shade to different heights and at random times. These ploys were designed to convince any would-be burglar that someone was always at home.

Albert's moving in with my parents removed any joy from their lives. He brooded constantly, and his countenance was one of a perpetual frown. He thought it was disrespectful to his departed mother if he were to smile or enjoy himself in any way. He refused to watch television or listen to music, and berated my mother for doing so. My father was not so easily manipulated, and would watch television in defiance of Albert, even if there were nothing he especially cared to see.

Mother and Dad liked watching the program *All in the Family*, the popular situation comedy featuring the bigotry of Archie Bunker and his constant bickering with his wife, daughter, and son-in-law. In those days, this program was innovative for including mild profanity and indelicate references of a sexual nature. Not wishing to be alone in his bedroom, where he might be beset with spooks or prying eyes from outside, Albert would come to the living room and find it difficult to avoid seeing the T.V. screen. He would occasionally smile at a humorous episode, but would immediately revert to his scowl, commenting on being ashamed for having smiled.

Albert was always prudish, and regarded much of *All in the Family's* humor as being unfit to watch. When I asked him why he watched such an offensive program, he said that he hated to admit it, but that it was funny.

Scottish people have a reputation for being thrifty, but if a competition were held to determine who were the most niggardly and penurious of all nationalities, it would be no contest if my German side of the family were candidates for this dubious honor. Albert's attitudes about his automobile, already mentioned, carried over to his behavior when he moved in with my parents; and his desire to save money was no stronger than my mother's.

The bathroom in my parents' home had a medicine cabinet with a mirror on its door, with an electric light on each side of the mirror. The two lights were operated with the switch on the wall. Each light also had its individual switch. As soon as I left the bathroom after shaving, my mother or Albert would rush in and turn off one of the switches at the mirror so that only one light would be lit when the wall switch was turned on.

When anyone went to the refrigerator, the door was not allowed to remain open for more than a second or two. Items had to be put in or taken out as quickly as possible in order to keep the light bulb inside from burning out prematurely.

My mother had an automatic wash machine for the laundry, but she would never allow it to run through its wash, rinse, and spin dry cycles. Instead, she would stop the wash cycle midway through, and put in another load of dirty clothes to save hot water and soap. She would then remove the washed clothes and rinse them by hand in stationary tubs. She had a clothes dryer, but would not use it. She always hung the clothes on a line out in the back yard, or in the basement if the weather were inclement.

Neighbors' homes were on each side of my parents' house. When our son was at my parents' house for a visit, and as he undressed to prepare for going to bed, he pulled down the window shade for privacy. When he awoke in the morning, dressed, and came to breakfast, my mother saw that the shade was down. She went into a rage, screaming at our son for having changed the height of the shade. Not only did she complain because the drawn shade made the windows appear unattractive, but more importantly, it would be worn out prematurely. She said that in all the years she had lived in the house, the shades had never been adjusted. When Albert adjusted the shade in his room upstairs (mentioned earlier as a security measure), she made it no issue, possibly because he was paying for room and board.

Virtually every home in the neighborhood had either central or individual room air conditioning. Her acquaintances convinced her to have a window air conditioner installed, almost a necessity in southern New Jersey's miserable, humid summers. She would not turn it on because of the electricity it used, but when I visited her, and wanted the AC turned on, she grudgingly allowed me to do so.

I had no brothers or sisters, but I had one cousin on my mother's side of the family, the daughter of my mother's brother, Alphonse. On my father's side, his brothers had no children, but his five sisters provided cousins. I addressed their husbands as "uncle" so-and-so, but my mother insisted that they were only related by marriage, and were not my "real" uncles. A few of these relatives, whether by blood or marriage, were not subjects for discussion in polite company. Cousin Artie, who was named after my father, became involved in burglary and served time in reform school. Cousin May, his sister, was a madam in a brothel. "Uncle" Sam was the manager of the world's light-heavyweight boxing champion; and when his fighter was dethroned, Sam managed a pool hall.

I mentioned earlier my father's leaving his hometown, and coming to New Jersey to avoid the draft. One of his friends, whom I shall refer to simply as George, came with him for the same purpose, and the two of them lived together in a boarding house in Camden. It astonishes me to this day that these men were friends for all their lives, despite the marked contrasts between them. As already alluded to, my father was never in trouble with the law as were his brothers; and he managed to remain law-abiding while associating with George, who was as dishonest as the day is long. Whenever George and my father went to a restaurant, and after finishing the meal, George always took the silverware and the salt and peppershakers with him.

George owned a motorcycle, and both men would ride together on the bike as recreation. On one particular outing, they were speeding down a country road and accidentally drove into a bump that threw the bike ten feet into the air. When they returned to earth, the bike landed in a narrow ditch that was several feet deep, and just wide enough to swallow up the bike. The riders, still seated, landed with their feet on each side of the ditch, and miraculously avoided injury.

In another motorcycle incident, George was riding with his brother, Joe, on a bike with a sidecar. They were in a farming area, and came to a pasture where sheep were grazing. The brothers thought that one of the animals would provide meat for the table. Luckily, there was a large gunnysack in the sidecar. They stopped, went into the field, grabbed the sheep, and stuffed it into the sack. They got back on the motorcycle and, within a few minutes, were pursued by a motorcycle policeman who was after them for speeding. Already having run-ins with the law, they had to avoid being caught with the stolen animal in their possession. The sheep was bleating loudly, and the sound was certain to get the cop's attention. They stopped when they were told to pull over, and Joe grasped the sack, squeezing the neck of the sheep that was inside. This stopped the animal's cries so that the theft was not detected. By the time the cop chatted with them and issued a ticket for exceeding the speed limit, the sheep died of asphyxiation.

After my father married, he remained a friend of Helen and Harvey at whose boardinghouse he and George had lived. They had no children, and when my mother and father took me with them to visit, I was bored silly. Helen was a marvelous cook, but a careless housekeeper; and I heard my mother make comments about Helen's house not being clean. I was getting tired, and lay on a davenport with my eyes shut. Harvey said, "It looks like Arthur's getting sleepy."

I replied, "No, I'm not. It's just the dust from Aunt Helen's rugs." I still recall my mother's trying to excuse my remark, saying that she couldn't imagine what possessed me to say such a thing!

Harvey and Helen had no income because of the Depression, and had no automobile. Helen's aged father, a widower, lived with two old cronies in impoverished conditions in a dilapidated farmhouse near Havre de Grace, Maryland. Helen had not seen her father for many years, and wanted desperately to visit him. My father took off a few days from work, and drove Helen, Harvey, my mother, and me to

Maryland for a little vacation.

I have hardly ever seen such poverty, before or since, under which Helen's father and his buddies lived. The ride from the main highway to the house was several miles on a rutted, dirt road. For me, as a little boy, it was a wonderfully wild, exhilarating adventure. Unlike Uncle Dave's farmhouse (discussed in the next chapter), their house had holes in the roof, and the steps leading to the porch were removed and used as firewood. Some time in the past, there was an explosion from something cooking in the kitchen, and the ceiling was splattered with greasy remnants that had never been removed. The window shades were torn from top to bottom, and the bed sheets had large holes in them.

There was no electricity, and the radio was battery powered. I recall Helen's father, his two buddies, Harvey, and my father listening to a broadcast by Father Coughlin, who gave weekly political messages shortly after FDR became President. The reception was full of static, and as young as I was, I would not have understood the subject matter even if the reception were clear.

The youngest of the three men living in the house—he was perhaps sixty years old—took me and their dog for walks around the farm. Nothing was cultivated; there were only wild grapes growing, and a cornfield with dried, empty stalks sticking up. We encountered a black snake, probably non-venomous and about three feet long, during our walk, and the dog grabbed it by the neck and shook it until it was dead. I related this exciting incident to my mother when we returned to the house, and she was horrified by the potential danger of snakes in the area. Using a penknife, the old guy fashioned an impressive whistle from a tree twig, and gave it to me. We also found a couple of box turtles, and Helen and I took them back to New Jersey as pets. Hers remained for many years in her little back yard that was enclosed with a wooden board fence. Not being able to confine mine, it escaped, and I was devastated at having lost a pet. Oddly, as I was walking home from school five years later, I found my turtle on the sidewalk a block away from my house. I recognized it as the same turtle because I had carved my initials on its shell when it lived in my yard.

Chapter 8
The Farm

As my mother pointed out to me, that relatives by marriage on my father's side of the family were not real relatives, the same was true also with non-blood relatives on her side. Thus, her aunt Amelia was married to David; and although I could call him "Uncle Dave," he was not to be thought of as my real uncle. I can state, parenthetically, that my relatives by marriage, and my in-laws, are frequently more to be admired, loved, and respected than those related by blood.

Uncle Dave was a poor German immigrant with no education whatsoever. He was a dear soul, and generous beyond measure. He lived on a five-acre farm, and being regarded as a country bumpkin, did not receive the respect that I felt he deserved. My most delectable childhood nostalgia is elicited by my memories of vacationing on his farm. How I reveled in feeding

Author on Uncle Dave's and Aunt Amelia's farm, 1927

the dog, chickens, pigs, geese, cow and horse!

The road by Aunt Amelia and Uncle Dave's house was not paved. It was just sand six inches deep, and automobiles struggled to keep from becoming bogged down. Uncle Dave did not own a car, but hitched the horse to a wagon when it was necessary to go into town; and it was, indeed, more expedient than using an automobile.

Author on farm with Aunt Amelia

I was born and reared in the suburbs, and experiencing the rustic life was a dream without compare. Lacking the ordinary comforts to which I had been accustomed was a treat: an outhouse instead of a bathroom, kerosene lamps and candles rather than electric lights, fireplaces instead of a furnace.

The farm was not very productive. Uncle Dave raised only a little corn, potatoes, and a few vegetables for their own use. I went with him as he brought the cow in from the meadow to the barn for milking. Being a small boy in proximity with such a large animal, I was afraid it might charge, as bulls are known to do. Seeking reassurance, I asked Uncle Dave what he would do if the cow were to charge at him. He replied simply, "I would bust her in the schnoot." I thought him to be a heroic figure because of his fearlessness.

*Author with Grampop on Uncle Dave's
and Aunt Amelia's farm, 1927*

To acquire items for the house or the barn at little or no cost, he would hitch his horse to the wagon and scavenge from the trash that would be deposited in front of houses in the city to be picked up by the local garbage trucks. Among his findings were toys that he saved for me when my parents visited once every five years or so. I remember well taking home with me a wagon, a kiddy-car, and toy automobiles made of cast iron. I played with these "treasures" for many years. These items were castaways when I got them; and when they wore out completely or were broken with use, my parents did not replace them with new ones. I cried bitterly when the front of my wagon collapsed, causing the wheels to fall off. I knew that my father was a master mechanic who could repair anything; but he never attempted to reattach the wheels, and I never had another wagon.

A football is something I really desired, but my mother wanted me to have nothing to do with a game where one was sure to become injured. Fortune smiled on me when I was given a football from Uncle Dave's scavenging. In those days, footballs were leather on the outside, containing a rubber bladder which was inflated by blowing it up by mouth. This particular bladder had a hole in it, and would not hold air; so I removed the bladder and stuffed the leather covering with leaves, packing them tightly. The football didn't bounce, and was rather squishy, but at least I had a football! I was in front of our house playing with it one early evening just as my father came home from work. I showed him how I had made the football playable without an air-filled bladder, and asked him to kick it. Knowing that Dad was athletic, I anticipated him to give it a mighty boot; and he did. It sailed perhaps thirty or forty feet into the air and struck the wires strung between the telephone poles by the street. I had never seen such a marvelous demonstration of physical prowess in my whole life. That anyone could kick a football high enough to hit those high wires was, to me, beyond belief!

Uncle Dave's picking up discarded trash had its limitations for furnishing his family's needs; so to supplement his income, he worked as a gravedigger at a cemetery eight miles from home. It wasn't practical to take the horse and wagon this distance every day, and the road, consisting of deep sand, did not lend itself to riding a bicycle, so he walked to and from work every day except Sunday.

His lack of education became evident on the occasion in which he wanted to sell two of his pigs. An acquaintance told him that he should sell them for twenty dollars apiece, and accept nothing less. A buyer came to look at them, and seeing that they were to his liking, told Uncle Dave, "I'll give you thirty dollars each."

Uncle Dave, remembering the advice he had been given, declared, "You can't cheat me! Twenty dollars or nothing!"

Chapter 9

Early Development

It is understandable that I was over-protected and not indulged, knowing my mother's frugality and caution. In later years I told my mother that some circumstances might have been handled differently, and had I been treated more like other kids, I would have been happier. Her response was that I grew up to be successful, proof that she did her job well. I realize, of course, that her doting on me, and being the disciplinarian that she was, had its benefits, and perhaps I ought not look back at my upbringing so critically.

Nobody believes me when I claim to remember being taken as an infant to a health clinic in my hometown. I vividly recall lying on a baby scale to be weighed, and was afraid I would fall off. Another early memory is of my being wheeled in my baby carriage. It was a wicker perambulator with a top that could be adjusted by rotating forward or backward as protection against the sun. This roof-like cover had small, round windows on the sides so that the carriage occupant could look out. I could not have been older than a year or two. I lurched forward and backward, and in response, my mother pushed the coach quickly forward and then brought it to a sudden halt, repeating this stop-and-go movement. This delighted me no end, I recall, but being too young to talk, I was unable to tell her to do it the next time I was taken in the coach. So on subsequent outings, I thrust myself back and forth as before in order to indicate I wanted another thrill ride.

I remember also the summer before going to kindergarten, at the age of four. How I envied the kids who walked past our house on their way to school, a building I had not yet seen. On the weekend before my first day of school, my parents invited "Uncle" Sylvester and "Aunt" Edith (whom I discussed in chapter 6) for a visit. I couldn't say "Edith," but called her "Eef." They were not related to us, but dear friends, and out of respect, I was made to call a number of our acquaintances "Uncle" or "Aunt" rather than using only their first names, or calling them "Mr." and "Mrs."

I eagerly anticipated the new experience of going to school, and was talking about it with our guests. Aunt Eef explained the protocol of getting the teacher's attention or responding to a question, by raising my hand before speaking in class. What a strange requirement, I thought! She also gave me the approved terminology of "number one" and "number two," when I needed to go to the boys' restroom. As it turned out, I learned that everyone knew the difference between the numbers, and we were not required to specify one function or the other.

On the first day of kindergarten, as well as every other day of the first school year, my mother walked to school with me and came for me at the end of the school day. No other child was accompanied to and from school as I was, and it was understandably an embarrassment for me. On the first day of class, the teacher showed us a jack-o'-lantern plant, which I had never seen before. She told us that its brilliant orange color was from Jack Frost's painting colors on leaves in the autumn. I thought that to be a ridiculous story.

Another kindergarten experience was one in which a toy airplane, showing its side view, was placed on the teacher's desk. We were given crayons and told to draw a picture of the airplane. I still remember my dilemma of trying to determine how I was to draw the plane's wing, which was jutting out towards the class. How could I depict a three-dimensional representation on a sheet of flat paper?

Another troublesome art assignment was to draw Santa Claus. There were crayons for the red suit, black boots, black belt, and blue eyes; but there was nothing with which to make a white beard. It did not occur to me to leave the page untouched to represent the white whiskers; I colored it with a light application of red, creating a pink beard! To my embarrassment, my classmates made fun of my portrayal of the jolly old fellow.

All little boys wore short pants in the first couple of grades; but Mother bought an outfit in the style of a Russian Cossack's uniform, which featured a long, flared blouse. To be sure, it was distinctive apparel, but my classmates responded to it by chanting, "Arthur's wearing a dress! Arthur's wearing a dress!" I cried because of their taunting, and when

I told Mother about it, she said that the kids were jealous of my outfit, and didn't recognize class when they saw it. Recognizing that I could not continue being ridiculed, she relented and allowed me to wear the usual type of clothing for that era.

When the weather was cold, and the short pants were not able to keep our legs warm, boys wore long stockings that were held up with garters attached to their underpants. Wishing to dress me in higher style than my classmates, Mother bought me silk underpants that went over the regular underwear. Unfortunately, they were longer than my outside short pants, and hung down below my pants so that everyone could see them. I would roll them up, but it was not long before they fell down and became visible for all to see.

This contributed to a particularly embarrassing chain of events when I was part of a class project depicting the development of a city. It took place on a sand table, which was a large sandbox on supports making it waist high. A group of boys carried wooden blocks about the size of building bricks, and set them up on the periphery of the table to resemble a wall around the city. After putting their blocks in place, these boys would bow from the waist and announce, "We are the builders."

Another group of boys, that included me, carried dollhouses about the size of large grocery bags found in supermarkets, and placed them a few feet apart within the walls erected by the builders. We would then take our bow and announce, "We are the architects."

Then the little girls would carry dolls to the table, lean them against the dollhouses, make a curtsy, and declare, "We are the mothers." We presented this show in an assembly attended by all the students and their parents. The program was enjoyed so well, that we were invited to present it at the high school, where hundreds of other students and their parents could see it.

On the night of the presentation I was wearing my long silk underwear, and as usual, it kept falling down below my short pants. I tucked the underwear up where it presumably could not be seen, then picked up my dollhouse to deposit on the table. As I walked across the stage in front of the full house of students and parents, the base of the dollhouse came loose, and was in the process of falling off completely. Recognizing that I was about to lose the bottom of the dollhouse, I tried to carry the house with one hand and to hold up the base with the other. At that moment, my silk underwear slipped down and was exposed for all to see, and I lacked a third hand to pull it up. Truly, this was one of my life's darkest moments!

Author's kindergarten class.
(Arthur, top row, third from right)

One day, as I was riding my kiddy-car (a small tricycle)—I was four or five years old—I saw three seven or eight year olds, Lester Dilks, Bobby Keck, and his brother, Donald, playing cowboys and Indians. The Keck boys' father was in prison for forgery. They wanted me to play with them, and I was pleased to be invited to be with these "grownups." After a few minutes I ran home crying, and my mother asked me what caused the red marks around my neck. I said that the kids wanted to hang somebody, and chose me. I didn't know what "hanging" meant, but when they tightened the noose around my neck, it hurt, and I pulled it off. That was close!

Lester was a spoiled only child. His toys, his electric trains—everything he owned—was elaborate and expensive. His father made an adequate living selling life insurance, but the family made no pretense of being in an elite social stratum. Because the Dilks ate supper at nine o'clock, they were considered to be enviable high society.

Whenever Lester, one of the boys who tried to hang me, came to my house, my mother always sent him home, feeling that he was potentially dangerous. He was not easily deterred, and he came over to our front porch one day carrying a black cloth bag. Ever keeping an eye on me, Mother asked him what was in the bag. He gave some noncommittal answer, but Mother insisted on seeing what was in the bag. Sheepishly, he took out a loaded revolver, saying that he was allowed to play with it. The sight of the weapon terrorized Mother, and she sent him home instantly. I do not know why my mother did not report to anybody—even the boy's mother—such incidents that could have led to lethal consequences.

As a little boy, I watched my father repairing our vacuum cleaner. When he removed the casing surrounding the motor, I saw sparks where the commutator contacted the brushes. The combination of the noise of the motor, the sight of blue fire, and the resulting smell of ozone, frightened me, and I would hide in another room when my mother vacuumed the rugs.

One day I was riding my tricycle, staying as ordered on the sidewalk and not going around the block. A furnace-cleaning truck drove up, and parked at the curb between me and where my house was located. A large, flexible hose two feet in diameter stretched from the basement of the house, where the furnace was located, to the truck, which had attached to it a gigantic cloth vacuum bag into which the furnace debris was blown. The bag sat on the street, and was perhaps six feet in diameter and ten feet long. The rush of wind coming through the hose distended the bag, and the motor's noise was thunderous. Truly, this was the mother of all vacuum cleaners!

I wanted desperately to go home to avoid this fearsome monster. Although I could clamber over the hose that crossed the sidewalk, I was unable to lift my tricycle over it. I was forbidden from going around the block to reach my house from the other direction, and I was not allowed to go out in the street to go around the parked vacuum cleaner truck.

A man came down the street and asked why I was crying, and I told him my problem. He said he would take me out in the street and around the truck, but I knew also that I was not permitted to go anywhere with strangers. What a predicament! Fearing that I would become lost if I went around the block—something I had never done before—I chose the option of going with the man. I told him that I was afraid of vacuum cleaners, and he told me to put my hand on the swollen vacuum cleaner bag and feel it. I was terrified of what might happen, but I felt it as suggested. My spirit was buoyed when I challenged this behemoth, and survived unscathed! Mother scolded me, however, for having gone in the street with a stranger. My proper action was to have waited until the furnace cleaner finished, and then I could go home.

I was no different from most kids who want a pet. Having no brothers or sisters, I felt that I deserved an animal companion. One evening I was out front of our house when Dad came home from work. He handed me a large carton, and told me to take it into the house, and be careful not to drop it. There were several holes about the size of a dime in the carton, and as I carried it, I felt something wet touch my finger. It never occurred to me, until I opened the box, that it was a puppy's tongue. What a delirium of joy! One of Dad's co-workers had a dog that produced a litter, and gave us one of the pups. I asked Dad what kind of dog it was, and he replied that it was a male dog. I misunderstood him to say "nail" dog. I rather liked the name; it had a good, masculine sound. When I told my friends and neighbors that it was a "nail" dog, strangely, no one had ever heard of that breed.

The dog wasn't housebroken, and when we let it go outside, it went next door into the yard belonging to Charlie and Minnie Gross. Mrs. Gross complained to Mother about stepping into the mess left by the puppy. Mother never liked animals, and with the added motive of wanting to keep peace with the neighbors, she persuaded Dad to get rid of the dog. I had had the dog for only a week, when I discovered it was gone. Mother said that it ran away, but I learned years later that Dad had taken it out into the country and abandoned it.

My experience with pets was no more successful when I was given a rabbit by another of Dad's co-workers. When it was brought home in a cage, it was sick. It just sat there and its head bobbed up and down in a slow, regular rhythm. I asked Dad whether it was a real rabbit, and he said it wasn't, and that its head moved because there was a spring in its neck. I soon discovered that its little round droppings indicated it was, indeed, a live rabbit.

I was always careful to pick it up by the ears, only to find out later that this was not the proper way of lifting a rabbit. I was young and casual about its care, and the rabbit died within a week. Dad took the dead animal to the back yard, dug a hole, and threw it in. I thought it should have been wrapped in a box or a cloth, or something, but it wasn't. The next day I filled the watering can and poured it on the gravesite. Our neighbor saw me watering the bare spot on the ground, and asked me what I was doing. I explained that my rabbit was planted there, and I was watering it so that it would grow into another rabbit. I envisioned a rabbit bush from which a rabbit would break loose when it became ripe!

Mr. Hanling, who operated a successful butter and egg business, owned the house where the furnace cleaning occurred. He was a dapper fellow who sported a pointed, waxed moustache, and drove a luxury Studebaker sedan, the swankiest car in the neighborhood. The city garbage and trash were collected at the curb twice each week, and Mr. Hanling took the containers of refuse to the curb without wearing any clothes whatsoever. His behavior was common knowledge in the neighborhood, but nothing was ever done to discourage him. People regarded his trash disposal routine as an amusing oddity. One morning a black man with a pushcart was scavenging the items on the curb, and saw Mr. Hanling coming out of his house without any clothes. He threw up his hands and cried, "Lordy, Lordy!" and ran off without his cart. Shortly afterwards the local newspaper published a story about a mysterious nudist colony on Grant Avenue.

Mrs. Hanling became seriously ill, and was confined to bed. It was the Fourth of July, and everyone shot off fireworks with impunity, there being no restrictions as to their potency. In the midst of the noisy celebration, Mr. Hanling came to everybody's house in the block, asking that we go elsewhere, because the sound of the explosions was disturbing his ailing wife. Dad took Mother and me, and one of my playmates, to an unpopulated wooded area outside of town. I was allowed to shoot off "ladyfinger" firecrackers, but Dad fired the big ones, not wanting me to be injured because of their potential danger. Mother sat alone in the back seat of the car, shooting my cap pistol. To avoid the sparks from the detonating caps, she held the pistol in front of her at arms length. One of the errant sparks flew up and struck the cloth ceiling, setting it ablaze. In an instant the entire overhead panel was in flames. She screamed, and we all ran to the car, smothering the flames with our hands. The fire was extinguished quickly, but the ceiling retained black smudges, and was unsightly for as long as we owned the car.

I was fortunate always to have a boyhood

friend in our immediate neighborhood about the same age, or a couple of years younger than I, with whom to play. Kenny Ralston was one such buddy whose mother was my mother's schoolteacher. Mother told me that her teacher, Mrs. Ralston, would stand in front of the class each morning, remove her dress, and put on another one for teaching the class. At day's end she changed her clothes again, undressing and dressing in view of the pupils.

Kenny had a pedal car that he would let me drive, and he would sit on the hood. I was allowed to go up and down the sidewalk on our block, and around the corner for a block, but I was not permitted to go completely around the block. I heard that a library was on the street parallel to ours, but never saw it because it would require me to continue around another corner, and that was prohibited.

One day while riding in Kenny's little car with Kenny on the hood, we came upon two uniformed policemen who walked a beat around the corner where there was a row of small businesses. One was known as "Nick, the Cop," and the other was an old German named Mr. Albrecht. Everyday they ambled along in front of the stores, ostensibly to keep the peace. As Kenny and I approached them, Nick barked out, "You can't drive an automobile with a passenger on the hood. You're under arrest!" He then took from his belt his "come-along" handcuff and put it around my wrist. It was the type of manacle with a handle that tightened its jaws when twisted. Nick twisted the handle, and the jaws squeezed my wrist, making me cry. He released me when I assured him I would never again carry Kenny on the hood.

When I told my mother about the incident, she gave me no sympathy. Rather, it worked to her advantage. Every afternoon she made me take a nap, and I never wanted one. She said that the policeman came by the house each day to make sure that all children take their naps. I was somewhat skeptical that this was true, but with a policeman's actually having "arrested" me, I would not dare let him find me awake during naptime!

Kenny's father was an army officer in World War I, receiving his commission after attending Bordentown Military Academy. Mother thought Mr. Ralston was handsome, and was impressed by his showing deference to a lady by standing when one came into his presence. My father did not demonstrate such overt chivalry, and Mother pointed out to me that military school turned out gentlemen of the highest order.

Kenny told me that his father was shot in the shoulder by a machinegun bullet in the war. I never knew anyone before who had been shot. Kenny's father took us bathing in the ocean, when I visited their rented cottage at the seashore one weekend, and he carried us separately on his back into the surf. As I climbed onto his back I saw the gouged-out wound in his shoulder, and almost revered him as a true-life hero. When Kenny and I played "war," we always grabbed our shoulder in pain when mimicking being hit by a bullet, and were never wounded elsewhere.

My father, being a machinist by trade, was always around motors of one kind or another, and I wanted to emulate him by having a motor of my own. I rummaged through some drawers of odds and ends in the basement and found different sizes and colors of wire, light switches, small gears, burned-out radio tubes, electric fuses, sockets, plugs, small metal boxes, and other miscellaneous junk, and created a gizmo that I declared to be a motor. I connected these items together to resemble a Rube Goldberg contraption, and set them on the windowsill in the kitchen. I proudly showed Kenny my creation, assuring him it was a real motor.

He went home and built a motor of his own; but when he showed it to me, I told him it wasn't a real motor because it didn't make any noise. He said that it was, indeed, a motor. He turned on a switch and hummed, imitating a motor sound. I told him that he was making the noise of a motor with his voice, because the motor stopped when he had to take a breath. He retaliated by wanting to see my motor again, and would prove that mine was also a fake. We went to my house, and I turned on my motor by pressing a button, and with my other hand below the windowsill, scratched its underside with my fingernails, creating a steady noise that did not stop when I breathed. He never caught on!

When I showed my mother the motor, she asked what it was for. She said that motors always had a purpose, and that they did something. Not having anything immediately in mind, I told her that it could do anything she wanted it to do. She said that she would like it to wash and dry the dishes. She went upstairs to do sewing, housecleaning, or whatever, and I did the dishes—something as a five or six year old I had never done before. In case she wanted to see the motor clean the dishes again, I explained that it operated only while I was at the controls, and nobody else could see it work.

Everybody in our entire block, on both sides of the street, knew everybody else. We were a close-knit neighborhood, and on summer evenings everyone went to his back yard or front yard and chatted with everyone else. Common causes helped bring families together. One such cause was the nuisance of thousands of birds that roosted in the Norway maples, buttonwoods, and poplar trees lining our street. The incessant din of their chirping annoyed most people, and the droppings of such a multitude of birds made a mess on the sidewalk.

The strategy to eliminate the birds was to prevent their roosting in the trees, and to accomplish this it would be necessary to frighten them away. Some of the neighbors had fireworks left over from the Fourth of July. Large firecrackers and sundry other explosives were set off; but there was no cessation of the birds' chirping, and they remained in the trees. Our next door neighbor, Bob Green, had a piece of angle iron about three feet long, and slammed it on the sidewalk. The clang from repeatedly smashing the iron to the pavement must have startled the birds, for they were suddenly completely silent. Their chirping was stilled, but they remained in the trees, and their messing the sidewalk remained unabated. I was still a kid, but for adults to resort to these antics seemed to me to be frivolous and silly.

Another project that elicited communal effort was aimed at ridding the neighborhood of cats that yowled throughout the night. The cats did not belong to anyone in our locality; therefore eliminating them by whatever means did not offend anyone.

The cats would stray from one back yard to another as dusk arrived. There was no attempt to kill them, but everyone wished merely to scare them so they would not return. Each neighbor chose his own unique method for preventing the cats from returning. Grampop was sitting on his back step with a BB gun. Charlie Gross, next door to him, had a cast iron door-stop in the shape of a turtle that he was prepared to throw at a passing feline. My father was next in line, and had a couple of bricks at the ready. Bob Green, at the next house, had a supply of Fourth of July torpedoes, the kind of device that exploded when thrown against the ground or any other hard surface.

Without further description, let it be said that each of the other neighbors all the way to the end of the block were prepared to assault the cats with some kind of missile if they came within range. As expected, a cat crept into a yard at the end of the row of houses. One neighbor after the other attacked the cat with his projectile of choice. The cat scurried unscathed from one yard to the next; and when it entered ours, my father ran towards it with a brick in each hand. Before he threw either brick, he stomped on the cat's hind leg. It howled, and with a limp, scurried out of sight. Never again did stray cats enter the neighborhood.

Chapter 10
Future Inklings

An incident that portended my professional future occurred when I was four years old. We had a beautiful old rosewood upright piano made by the *Rudolph Company* in New York. My grandfather gave it to my mother when she was twelve years old. She took it to her home when she married, and having had a few lessons as a child, was able to play a few simple pieces as relaxation from housework. I didn't especially enjoy her music, and regarded the instrument as a curio on which I would occasionally bang out some meaningless noise.

My father and mother were upstairs one evening getting dressed to go out and visit friends. I was already dressed and sat in the living room, waiting for them. Something—whatever it was has long since been forgotten—prompted me to go to the piano. Without saying anything I stood at the keyboard and played the melody to *America* without missing a note. My mother, upstairs, hollered down, "Who's playing the piano?"

I would like to report that I responded with, "It is I, Mother," but more than likely, I merely said, "It's me, Mamma!" For some unknown reason, I was able spontaneously to discern that the distance between the keys was related to the melodic intervals of the song, and played the complete piece without hesitation.

I began by playing on the middle C key. Had I begun on any other key, the tune would, of course, have been incorrect, unless I used one or more black keys as appropriate. My random selection of the correct key on which to begin was, indeed, fortuitous. From that time on I continued to "pick out" tunes with which I was familiar, but was not introduced to formal piano lessons until I was almost eight years old. My piano teacher was Mary Goodyear. She came to our house and charged fifty cents for a half hour lesson. Soon thereafter, she gave up teaching when she married, and I went to the Fuhrman School of Music in Camden.

Lessons cost a dollar, but because Miss Goodyear had been a student at the school, I was charged only fifty cents. Miss Fagan was my teacher, and she earned most of her income by playing with a combo in a nightclub in Philadelphia. My mother invited her to visit our home one evening, but my father left the house before she arrived. He disapproved of her because, as a cabaret entertainer, she had a tainted reputation.

As a young piano student I was without nerves, and played regularly for recitals at the school, and for numerous clubs and social functions in the community, and a newspaper columnist wrote that I was a prodigy with rare ability. Ever ambitious for putting me in the limelight, my mother took me for an audition to perform on a German language radio program over station WRAX in Philadelphia. I was nine years old, and played for broadcasts every week for several months. Not yet knowledgeable in the German language, I knew to go to the piano because I heard the announcer say my name. For one of the programs I played a bombastic, but banal, composition entitled *Qui Vive*. I received the customary applause from the live audience, and the German-speaking announcer said something immediately after I finished playing. The audience responded to his comments with even more enthusiastic applause. Not understanding German, I asked my mother later why there was extra clapping, and she said that the announcer remarked how extraordinary it was for such a young performer to play this technically difficult tour de force.

Author in 1933, at age 9, when he performed as pianist on weekly radio broadcasts.

My cousin Alberta also took piano lessons, but had little musical talent. Her father, my uncle Al, showed a nasty attitude towards my "showing up" his daughter, and told family members mockingly that I played over station WR ich kutz, rather than WRAX. "Ich kutz" is German slang for "I throw up."

I told one of my teachers, Mrs. Ellis, that I played *Qui Vive* on the radio show. I pronounced it, "Kwee Veevay," because my mother had told me that this was the correct French title. Mrs. Ellis was fluent in French and offered the proper pronunciation, "Key Veeve," and when I told my mother that my teacher gave me the true pronunciation, my mother denounced Mrs. Ellis for being snooty, and spoke disparagingly of her thereafter.

As a child I went to Sunday school regularly, earning lapel pins for several years of perfect attendance. Mother and Father remained in bed until noon, and without prompting, I would wash, dress, eat breakfast, and walk the couple of blocks to St. Luke's Lutheran Church. The accepted age of accountability was thirteen, and the pastor suggested that I enroll in catechetical class in preparation for confirmation. I attended his class once each week, and was confirmed on the Palm Sunday following my fourteenth birthday. My mother and father attended the ceremony; and it was the first time in my memory that Father went to church. Even Uncle Bert, although a skeptic despite having been confirmed as a child, was present. The shallowness of his own spirituality was evident by his saying that, during prayer, he held his head high proudly, rather than bowing as did all the hypocrites in the congregation. He asked me what change in myself I had experienced as a result of the confirmation ritual. I can only suppose he felt gratified that I did not express any noticeable superiority with my becoming officially a church member.

Author with parents on confirmation day, 1939

After confirmation, the teenage members were automatically enrolled in Luther League, a church-related youth group devoted to wholesome social activities. Our meetings were held at the church on Friday evening, and lasted for an hour between six and seven o'clock. I no longer remember what activity occurred one evening, but I was at the church until nearly 7:15 p.m., and did not arrive home as early as expected. I was walking home with one of the other newly confirmed children, and as we passed by the business district—where I knew all of the proprietors—I met my mother, who was virtually running to find out why I was late arriving home. She screamed at me and spanked me, swatting my bottom all the way down the street, in view of my friend and the shopkeepers. To be physically punished publicly at the age of fourteen was a humiliation that I have never been able to eradicate from my mind.

During the years before being confirmed, I usually took part in the Christmas pageants. The director of these dramatic functions was a dear lady by the name of Miss Kammerhof. Financial resources were sparse, and make-do provision for costumes and scenery was a necessity. For one particular Christmas show, I was cast as a lowly shepherd in Bethlehem's fields. I wore a costume fashioned from a burlap bag, and my legs were wrapped in burlap strips. I didn't know their purpose other, perhaps, than representing a poor man's stockings in those ancient times.

I was walking back and forth across stage to depict traveling to the town where the Christ child was lying in a manger. While on my "journey," the swaths of leg wrappings came undone and unraveled behind me, and I had to stop and retrieve them to keep from tripping over them.

The lack of money for such dramatic productions also precluded proper stage lighting, so Miss Kammerhof used infrared heat lamps borrowed from congregation members to serve as spotlights. The illumination was far from adequate, and the heat was unbearable, causing the actors who were garbed in heavy, rough gunnysacks to sweat profusely.

The next year I was not to be in the Christmas pageant, but right before the evening's performance, one of the kids who played the part of one of the Magi bringing frankincense to the baby Jesus became suddenly ill. A quick substitute had to be found, and I was chosen to fill the vacancy. It was a speaking part, which although not very long, contained several lines which I was supposed to learn in a few minutes. I practiced and practiced intensively so that I could say my part without stumbling over the words. I was to hold a jar of frankincense in my hands, and while presenting it to the babe in the manger, describe my gift and express my adoration for the Savior.

Given such short notice, try as I might, I could not recite my lines without making blunders. Then a brilliant ploy came to me! I would simply attach a piece of paper, containing my lines, to the inside of the draping sleeve of my royal robe. I believed that, by holding out the jar of frankincense with the *outside* of my sleeve towards the audience, I could look at my prompt sheet pinned to the *inside*, and read it without fear of forgetting my words. I strode confidently across stage to the manger, but to create an effective night scene, the stage lights were turned off. The only illumination was that of a candle in the stable, which was totally useless for enabling me to read my script. Unable to see the note pinned to my sleeve, I improvised the essence of my prescribed lines as well as I could, mentally vilifying whoever might be responsible for creating the dramatic night scene, resulting in a less-than-perfect performance.

I had more success in "dramatic" activities

in the public school. Miss Leeds, our fourth grade teacher, directed a minstrel show featuring boys in the fourth, fifth, and sixth grades. It was patterned after the black face minstrel shows that were popular on stage and radio in the 1930's. White men put on these professional shows, and were made to look like Negroes by applying burnt cork to their faces. Entertainment that portrayed black people as being naively stupid was not uncommon in those days; and the popular radio program, *Amos n' Andy*, was one such example.

Author's boy classmates, 1934. Minstrel show members, Arthur (top row, third from right); Walter Reckard (top row, second from right); Bill Wheeler (bottom row, second from left); Helga Johnson (bottom row, third from left); Tom Cowgill (bottom row, third from right); and Charles Casper (bottom, second from right).

Our elementary school version included typical minstrel personalities such as interlocutor, or middleman, and was played by Tom Cowgill. Charles Casper and Walter Reckard were the end men, so called because they were at each end of the first row and told jokes. The rest of the group sang songs. A boy would sing as soloist a popular song of that era, and the whole group would sing it again. I was the soloist for one of the "hit" tunes at that time entitled *I'm Sitting High on a Hilltop.* Its lyrics continued, "Tossing all my troubles to the moon; where the breeze seems to say, 'Don't you worry.' Things are bound to pick up pretty soon."

Another crowd-pleaser contained the words, "Oh, gimme a horse, a great big horse, and gimme a buckaroo; and let me 'Wahoo, wahoo, wahoo!'" Some of the parents thought the show to be mildly scandalous when we sang the popular tune, *Sweetie Pie,* and each boy put an arm around a little kindergarten girl standing at his side.

One of the jokes was the old one about a fellow who was in the hospital for surgery. When he came out of the anesthesia he noticed that the window shades in his hospital room were pulled down, and asked why. The nurse told him that there was a fire across the street, and if he saw it he may have thought the operation was not a success. The audience roared with laughter, but I didn't "get it." After I came home after the show, my mother explained that the patient might think he was in h-e-1-1. She always spelled, rather than said, words that were forbidden for me to say. Further, she said it was a naughty story because of its implication, and it should not have been told.

The boys were told to wear white pants as a costume, and everybody had a pair except me. A father of one of the boys, Bill Wheeler, had been in the navy during World War I, and still had his white uniform, and let me wear it. That I was not small for my age is attested to by the fact that the uniform fit me, a ten-year-old.

At one of our rehearsals the teacher asked a couple of the boys to roll the small upright piano to another part of the room. They moved it too vigorously and it toppled over, fracturing the ankle of Helga Johnson, one of the boys in the show.

The fact that we could put on a minstrel show with impunity reflected the racial bias that prevailed at the time. Blacks—we referred to them as "colored"—were not permitted to live in our town. There was a lovely park in town named after a well-to-do businessman who donated the land. His will stipulated that Knight's Park would no longer belong to the borough if any colored people were allowed to live in Collingswood.

One of my playmates was a little girl named Betty Barry, who lived a few houses from ours. One day we were playing on the sidewalk, and a black man was walking towards us. He was just a visitor, possibly on his way to mow somebody's lawn, or for whatever reason. After he passed by us, Betty said to me, "Do you realize that he might be just as good as us human beings?" In view of the prevailing attitude concerning racial prejudice, I thought that her comment was gracious, and I averred that I, too, felt he might be our equal.

Author with Betty Barry, 1928

Whatever misbehavior I exhibited as a young child—or even through my teenage years—was never of a serious nature that might worry my parents. In the section of the report card which dealt with conduct, I frequently received a checkmark in the box alongside "Whispers too much." On one occasion I pushed my way in front of a little girl, Ruth Aaron, not allowing her to go ahead of me down the aisle between the rows of desks. Because of this unmannerly behavior, the teacher indicated on my report card that I was "rude and discourteous." My mother reprimanded me harshly upon seeing my report card, and brought this incident to my attention for years to come whenever she was displeased with me for any reason.

When we were taught phonics in an early reading class, each pupil took a turn to say a letter of the alphabet, and followed with a word beginning with that letter. One child said, for example, "'A' is for 'apple.'" The next one might say, "'B' is for 'ball.'" When it was my turn to recite, the letter was "H." I said, "'H' is for 'hooch.'" This was the Prohibition Era, and I had heard the next-door neighbor, Mr. Gross, say the word, but I didn't know what it meant.

The teacher, Miss Griscom, said to me, "That's not very nice, Arthur!" She sent me home with a note to inform my mother about what I said, and my mother came to school and tried to convince the teacher that "hooch" was not a term that was used in our house.

In Miss Heine's third grade spelling class, we were to say a word, spell it, and use it in a sentence. The word assigned to me was "sake." I said, "Sake. S-A-K-E. For heaven's sake, don't do that again!"

Miss Heine remonstrated, "One must not use Bible terms. That's swearing!" She then asked George Allen to make an acceptable sentence.

George replied, "For gracious sake, don't do that again!"

She complimented George and said, "That's

much better!" I did not realize that I was using profanity, and was absolutely crushed!

My scholastic grades were always very good except in penmanship. I resisted following the writing techniques demanded by the Palmer method. This discipline required holding the pen so that it rested between the thumb and against the third joint of the first finger. The hand rested on the fingernails of the fourth and fifth fingers, allowing it to glide across the paper. The fingers were not to move; rather, the arm was to rotate on its fleshy part as it rested from wrist to elbow on the desk. To achieve facility in this technique, we were assigned various kinds of writing calisthenics, as it were, such as making ovals retracing each other, and inserting vertical push-pull lines inside them. As we executed these patterns in rhythmic cadence, we would recite, "Hippity-hop to the candy shop to buy a stick of candy. One for you, and one for me, and one for Uncle Andy."

Penmanship class was taught through several years of elementary school. Every pupil had to complete a workbook of exactly duplicated upper and lower case letters of the alphabet, as well as arbitrary writing acrobatics. Weeks were required to finish the assignment, and when it was completed successfully, a lapel stickpin and a certificate were awarded. I received this recognition only once, but I cheated when the teacher wasn't watching, by "drawing" my letters, rather than creating them with the presumably elegant procedure prescribed by Mr. Palmer.

In addition to the shameful marks on the report

card for whispering and rudeness, my attendance record showed that I was frequently late for school. Classes started at 8:45 a.m., and I would be awakened at 8:00 a.m. Clearly, this did not allow enough time to wash, dress, eat breakfast, and walk three blocks to the school. I do not know why I was not made to get out of bed earlier, especially since my mother was such a strict disciplinarian. Listening to the radio contributed to my tardiness; its distraction interfered with my eating and dressing. I listened to a silly fifteen-minute program called, "Jolly Bill and Jane," which featured mildly adventurous episodes about a father and his little daughter; and I also enjoyed a program by a Japanese xylophone player. Such dallying caused me frequent misery, because of the embarrassment of entering the classroom alone after the late bell rang, and the class's being already in session.

One of the favorite radio programs of the 1930's was the Major Bowes Amateur Hour. My mother frequently expressed the desire for me to compete, but traveling to New York meant a financial burden that was unthinkable. A similar, although less significant, amateur competition took place at Camden's Convention Hall in 1936. It was held in conjunction with an exhibit of new automobiles. The amateur show participants included singers, imitators, instrumentalists of various kinds, and a cross-eyed young woman, clad in a skimpy, revealing two-piece outfit, who tap danced wearing roller skates. I was the only pianist in the contest, and I played *Liebestraum*, by

Franz Liszt. The winner of the contest was to be determined by whoever received the most applause. There were several thousand people in the audience. When the contest ended, the emcee stood behind each contestant and, as he held his hand over our heads, the audience applause was recorded on an applause meter. I received an impressive response, and believed that I would be declared the winner. When the emcee put his hand over the head of the cross-eyed, skimpily clad dancer on roller skates, the applause was deafening! She was the undeniable winner, and she didn't even keep time with the music! I vowed then and there never to enter another amateur contest, and I didn't!

After the contest my mother and I looked at the new cars, and I was especially impressed with the Cord. Its price was twenty-two hundred dollars, and it was the most sleek and unique car I had ever seen, with its retractable headlights, exhaust manifolds exiting as long tubes from the sides of the hood, front-wheel drive, and toggle-switch gear shift mounted on the dashboard.

There was a poster, along with other incidentals in the arena, with "SOS" in large letters. The letters preceded the words, "Stamp Out Syphilis." I blurted out, "Mamma, what's syphilis?" She shushed me, and said that she would tell me later. When we got home, she said that syphilis was a disease that affected bad people. I knew that I was not always well behaved, and asked whether I could get syphilis. Mother said

I did not have to worry, but did not explain why. I was also ordered never to say the word, and I didn't understand this, either.

Chapter 11

Hard Times

It's necessary at this point to take my narrative back just a few years to the "Great Depression." Many of our neighbors were unemployed, but my father always had steady work at the Cork Works, making more than average salary. Despite his relatively fortunate financial situation, frugality was the byword that guided our mode of living. We did not have a telephone in the house until 1940. Grammom, who lived two houses from us, had a telephone that was paid for by Uncle Bert. Whenever we wanted to use a telephone, we went to Grammom's to make the call. The next-door neighbor, between our house and Grammom's, didn't have a telephone, either, and she felt no qualms about asking to use it whenever she wanted to make a call.

Father gave Mother ten dollars each week to buy food and pay for my piano lesson. My parents complained whenever I required new shoes. When holes would appear in the soles, I would cut a piece of cardboard to size and insert it inside the shoe. When it rained or snowed, it took no time at all for my feet to become soaked, resulting in my having frequent coughs and fever.

When the cardboard inserts became patently inadequate for protecting my feet, I was sent to the store to buy a repair kit containing rubber soles and glue to patch the shoe bottoms. The glue lacked sufficient adhesion to hold the soles securely, and rain or snow leaked between the patches and the shoes. Again, as incongruous as it may appear, I feel to this day that my parents valued having me as their child, but did little to accommodate some of my basic necessities. I never owned a raincoat, a pair of rubber overshoes, or an umbrella; so when the weather was inclement, I was always drenched to the skin, and sat chilled all day at school. I really envied my classmates, who, despite their parents' suffering the woes of the depression, dressed adequately to keep warm and dry. Nowadays, most people who are not feeling well stay home from school or from work, but I attended school many days with a sore throat, chills, and fever.

When I was an infant, and still being bottle-fed, I was given Eagle Brand milk. Still available today, it is condensed milk made viscous by the addition of sugar. The result of this unhealthful formula was that my baby teeth were black and rotted near the gum line. A teenage girl named Angie, who was the daughter of the local barber, asked my mother why she didn't brush my teeth. I was terribly embarrassed by my appearance, and my mother told Angie that she was impudent. When my mother went to have her teeth filled by a dentist in Camden, I always went with her on the bus. The dentist never examined my teeth, despite their horrible condition; but as my baby teeth began to fall out, my mother asked the dentist to pull one of the back molars that was partly broken. I protested, not wanting to have an extraction, but Mother told me that the dentist was just going to "look" at the tooth. When I got in the chair, the dentist sneaked his forceps in my mouth without my seeing them, and pulled the tooth. Mother reprimanded me for complaining, saying that baby teeth had no roots, and there could not have been any pain.

As my teeth progressively loosened, my parents would try to hurry the process by tying a string around each one to eliminate it, rather than allowing it merely to fall out. I would not let them pull one of the teeth that had become loose, so my father laid me on my back on the davenport, sat on my chest, and tried to pull the tooth with his fingers. I cried and fussed furiously, and he slapped me across the face repeatedly until he finally extracted the tooth. Mother stood by, watching, and telling my father to relent, but he ignored her. My face was full of black and blue welts from the beating, and Mother told me later that he vowed never to hit me again. He lived up to his promise to her, but never said anything to me about it.

My mother was a very affectionate person, lavishing hugs and kisses on me and on my father. She sobbed noticeably when watching a sad motion picture, or listening to a touching radio program, or when leaving friends or family who lived far away. Father was always the stalwart one, and never cried as long as I knew him. I thought of him as the paragon of masculinity, and showed heartfelt affection for him, but he never returned my hugs or kisses. Neither Father nor Mother ever read to me. The only books I had were an alphabet book, given to me when I was about two years old, containing pictures corresponding to each letter, such as "A is for Apple, B is for Boat, etc."; an illustrated collection of *Mother Goose Rhymes* about "Jack Sprat, Little Miss Muffet, Old Mother Hubbard, etc.," and three books in the series about *Buster Brown and His Sister Sue*, given to me by "Uncle" Bob and "Aunt" Esther, the next-door neighbors. I glanced at these latter books, but the subject matter seemed too juvenile for my taste, and I never read them.

Like most boys, I liked guns; and like many mothers, mine hated them. After much pleading, I was allowed to order a wooden replica of the revolver used by movie and radio hero, Tom Mix. Many kids' items in those days were available by mailing two box tops, or one box top and ten cents, to a cereal manufacturer. I never had the patience to wait until I ate two whole boxes of cereal, so I opted for sending the dime and one box top. After the usual six to eight-week wait, the treasured gun arrived. It was a remarkable likeness; it was actual size, and the cylinder rotated like the real thing.

I was across the street with my new gun, playing with two of my friends, Billy and Carl Eisenberg. My mother called me to come home, but because of the distance and our making a lot of racket at play, I didn't hear her. She came to get me, and was so furious that I did not come home when she called, that she snatched my treasured toy, and slammed it to the ground, smashing it into splinters.

Billy and Carl lived in a house that had a shed in the back, used for garden tools. Having a clubhouse—an improvised shelter of one kind or another—was popular and normal for kids during that era. The three of us decided to form our own club, and call it the ABC Boys, representing our first initials for Arthur, Billy, and Carl. When I announced being in a club, my mother screamed, "No club!" I thought that by waiting for my father to come home, I might get a more reasonable response, but he echoed her opinion.

When I asked why I could not join a club, Mother and Father both agreed that bad people belong to clubs. I asked, "What about Mr. Henderson and Mr. Shurtleff? They belong to the country club." These were perfectly honorable family men who lived in our immediate neighborhood, so I thought I had a winning argument. Without a moment's hesitation, both of my parents declared that clubs are evil, no matter who belonged to them. Discussion closed.

Mother would play board games with me, but Father never spent time with me except grudgingly "playing catch" in the back yard for a few minutes after supper in summer. Because he worked hard all his life, spending time just for fun was foreign to him. He never went fishing or hunting with or without me, and never engaged in any hobbies or joined me in any activities. His only interest was gardening, and after supper he would tend his roses and tomato plants.

After opening his machine shop, as I described earlier, his gardening was essentially abandoned. Upon completing an eight-hour day at Armstrong Cork Company, he worked at his shop until midnight or later, including weekends.

While I was in junior and senior high school, I was in many musical activities, including the orchestra, band, choir, boys' glee club, and played the piano as soloist and as accompanist for various vocalists and instrumentalists. There were daily assemblies, and I would play the piano for the singing that was led from the stage by Miss Paxon. The assemblies in junior and senior high schools comprised approximately seven hundred students, and they sang a variety of folk and art songs as well as popular hymns. There were the seasonal carols at Christmas and Easter, and throughout the year there would be such unabashedly Christian hymns such as *Holy Spirit, Truth Divine*; *Holy, Holy, Holy*; *Lead On, O King Eternal*; *O Worship the King*, and *Come, Thou, Almighty King*. There were not more than a half dozen pupils in the entire student body who were Jewish, and no animosity was expressed by Jews or unbelievers about singing these kinds of pieces.

My mother attended programs in which I was a participant occasionally, but she often could not go because she did not drive, and my father was not home to take her. It was a mile between home and school, and I always walked both ways. I recall my father's being at one program when I was in the seventh grade, and he attended my junior high graduation ceremony with my mother and a neighbor lady, Mrs. Gross.

For this occasion all of the girls were required to wear white dresses, and the boys had to wear white trousers and dark jackets. Every boy had white "duck" trousers, but I did not. By the time I was in ninth grade, every boy in the class except me and Bill Sheppard wore long trousers; we continued to wear knickers. My first long trousers were hand-me-downs from Uncle Bert, and he loaned me his white wool flannels for the graduation ceremony. It was beastly hot that day, and I was tormented by the scratchiness of wool on my legs.

As a special feature of the program I played a difficult piano transcription by Franz Liszt on Schubert's song, *Hark! Hark! The Lark.* Until this time I was always eager to perform in public, and was never nervous. For this occasion I suffered wretchedly with anxiety, because of anticipating an audience of close to a thousand people.

At each graduation the American Legion awarded a medal to the outstanding boy who best demonstrated the qualities of honor, courage, scholarship, leadership, and service. I was the recipient of the award in 1939, and it was one of the proudest moments in my mother's life. My father, as was typical, had nothing to say, but when we arrived back home, he handed me an envelope. Inside I found a twenty-dollar bill! I thanked him for it, as it was a lot of money in those days. He said, "You better look a little deeper." I re-examined the envelope and found two more twenties! My mother said that she had no idea that my father was giving me a gift.

When I was in high school he came to two concerts at which I accompanied Howard Vanderburg, the leading baritone of the Philadelphia Opera Company. He sang an impressive program with demanding piano accompaniments. At its conclusion he reached over the grand piano to shake my hand in appreciation and congratulation, and my mother spoke about the thrill of this moment with acquaintances for years thereafter. Dad also attended my high school commencement and, unusual for him, expressed pride for my receiving an award never before offered, in recognition of my three years of musical contribution to the school. The announcement of my winning a scholarship to Temple University also gave him reason to be pleased. Without it, I would have been unable at that time to continue my education.

Chapter 12

The Cadet

It is necessary at this point to reverse the chronology a bit, and go back a year. In the summer following my junior year in high school I was sixteen years old, and was invited to be a cadet at Wanamaker Camp in Island Heights, New Jersey. All employees of the John Wanamaker department store in Philadelphia were required to spend their summer vacation at the camp. Two weeks were provided for the men and two weeks for the women. If an employee chose not to attend camp, preferring to spend his vacation elsewhere, he received only one week off. America had not yet entered the war, and jobs were at a premium, and one did not want to jeopardize his employment by not going along with the management's arbitrary vacation arrangements.

The father of one of my classmates worked at the store, and having heard me play the piano for school concerts, asked me to be the camp pianist. There was a big sendoff as we marched down Market Street in Philadelphia before boarding buses to take us to camp.

The camp was operated like a genuine military academy. Everyone in the Philadelphia metropolitan area knew about the camp, and regarded Wanamaker cadets as being special, as though they were in one of the real service academies. There was no justification for this opinion other, perhaps, than the camp's being conducted in a "spit and polish" manner, and having a strictly enforced code of military regulations. Failure to obey could result in being fired from the company.

The camp comprised companies, platoons, and squads headed by officers and noncoms; and Percival Jones, a retired army captain from World War I, commanded the entire operation. He wore jodhpurs and puttees, and carried a swagger stick; everyone was terrified of him. Officers were saluted, and inspections of our tents, equipment, and appearance occurred daily. We wore sharp uniforms not unlike those worn at West Point or Annapolis. A bugler announced daily events, such as reveille, mess call, retreat, taps, and tattoo. Every evening there was dress parade that drew large crowds who came from town to see us. We marched, carrying vintage rifles that were rendered inoperative by the removal of their firing pins. Two bands provided the music. One used standard band instruments, and the other comprised drummers and bagpipers, attired in kilts and other Scottish paraphernalia.

For several weeks before camp, I was required to go to the Philadelphia Wanamaker store to be taught the manual of arms, close order drill, and show routines that took place in the evening parades. This knowledge proved to be useful later when I entered the army. Being already familiar with marching directives and manipulating a rifle, I assisted in teaching recruits these disciplines at my first basic training camp.

Author in Camp Wanamaker cadet uniform, 1940.

Still in high school, and being considerably younger than the other cadets, I was intimidated by the imposed military regulations, and grownup talk about short arm inspections, going out on the town after hours, and other such adult ventures.

The men perceived that I was naïve, and told me to make the evening report to the camp commander. I had to go to his quarters, salute him, and state that all in my platoon were "present and accounted for." I did not realize at the time that many of the men went into town to pick up girls or visit the saloons, and I was covering for them.

Everybody in the camp was required to engage in an athletic activity. I never participated in high school sports, and knew I would be at a disadvantage competing with grown men in baseball, softball, rowing, or track and field events. I did, however, have experience in archery, which was one of the activities available. Back home I used to go to the city dump with friends who also had bows and arrows, and shoot rats and red-winged blackbirds. Subsequently, I became quite a good shot.

I owned a good, custom-made lemonwood bow and quality arrows, but the equipment provided at the camp was inferior and not well maintained. A tournament was held, and having the highest score of all other competitors, I expected to be given a medal at the awards ceremony at the last night of camp. Seeing the opportunity to have fun with me as a young guy among the older cadets, an announcement was made that my winning the medal was being held in abeyance, because another person wanted to participate in the tournament, but was unable to because he had been involved with another event at the same time as the archery competition. Furthermore, he was said to be an expert with much experience. I was disheartened at the possibility of having this latecomer winning the medal to which I felt entitled.

He was allowed to compete the next day. I watched anxiously as he placed the arrow on the string, and drew it back; but he held the bow horizontally rather than in the customary vertical position. There were a few snickers and smiles among the onlookers, and I realized that an attempt was being made to play a trick on me. It was evident that this fellow knew nothing about archery because of his unorthodox technique.

He released the arrow and, as luck would have it, he scored a dead center bull's eye! I was devastated! He placed another arrow to the bowstring and shot; and another, and another. Every shot fell wide of the mark, with several arrows missing the target entirely. Everyone had a good laugh, and it was later revealed that this whole episode was calculated as a prank. I won the first-place medal fair and square!

People are understandably disbelieving when somebody swears to have seen a rare or strange phenomenon such as an unidentified flying object, or the Loch Ness monster, for example. One morning I awoke early, perhaps five o'clock or thereabouts, and took a walk to Tom's River which abutted the camp. No one else was astir, and I was alone, looking out at the river. Suddenly, I saw a disturbance on the water, and breaking the surface was a serpentine figure, its looping sections rising and falling as it swam only a hundred feet or so from where I was standing. It appeared to be perhaps twelve to fifteen feet long. There was no discernible head, per se, but just an undulating tubular body, traveling the speed of a walking person. Staring in disbelief, and not knowing what it was, I literally and purposefully pinched myself to be certain I was awake, and not dreaming. I first noticed it at quite some distance to my left, and observed it for the full minute or two required for it to pass finally out of sight at the right.

It was years later before I mentioned this incident to anyone. As a matter of fact, I think that I told no one except my wife some time after we were married. When anyone today divulges having seen an oddity that is completely far-fetched, he is rarely believed, and is regarded as being "a few cards short of a deck." I recognized, even as young as I was, that my reputation for being rational would be in serious doubt, had I said anything publicly about this weird occurrence.

Chapter 13

The Call

My parents were traditionally Republicans, but with the successful end of the Great Depression, they were staunch supporters of Franklin Delano Roosevelt. With the prospect of America's getting into the war that was already raging in Europe, there was talk of drafting eighteen year olds into the military, and this reduced my parents' enthusiasm for FDR's policies.

On December 7, 1941, I was still sixteen years old. I was listening to the radio, and the New York Philharmonic Orchestra, with pianist Artur Rubinstein, were performing Brahms' *Second Piano Concerto*. As a serious music student, I was avidly delving into all the major composers, and Brahms topped my list of favorites. In the midst of the concert, my parents decided to look for greenery to be used as decoration for Christmas, which was only a couple of weeks away. Fortunately, our 1936 Dodge had a radio, so I was able to hear the program while away from the house. We went to the nearby town of Haddonfield that had a parkway where shrubs and trees abounded. My father parked the car and walked a short distance to some evergreen bushes. He broke off a few sprigs and took them back to the car. The radio program was interrupted by the announcement

that Pearl Harbor was attacked. I was as annoyed
with the concerto's being interrupted as I was with
our being at war.

I was too young to be drafted or enlist, and
recognized that my going into military service was
inevitable. I could face it with equanimity, but it was
a dire prospect that made my mother inconsolable.
We returned home with the decorative twigs, and
a few days later a registered letter arrived containing a summons—with the option of paying a stiff
fine—for defacing and stealing public property. A
police patrol apparently drove past our parked car,
saw my father purloining the greens, and took down
the license number. Rather than recognizing this as
an infraction of the law, my parents saw no reason
why they could not, with impunity, help themselves
to the free, available ornamental greenery; but they
paid the $30 fine.

As soon as I graduated from high school, at
age seventeen, I got a summer job working in the
office of a sheet metal plant, which was manufacturing bulkheads for naval vessels. My duties consisted
of taking care of time cards, filing papers, and delivering messages to various parts of the factory such
as the stock room, the welders, and other groups of
workmen. I planned to enter Temple University in the
fall, but was not honest enough to tell my employer,
because of his likely reluctance to hire someone on
a temporary basis. My hourly wage was $18.40 per
week, and thirty-six cents was taken out for Social
Security. Of the $18.04 take-home pay, my father

told me to give my mother ten dollars each week for room and board; this left $8.04 for my personal use.

At summer's end I enrolled in the university as a music education major. For my own benefit, as well as trying to solace my mother over the looming draft, I tried to enter the navy R.O.T.C. that was available on campus. I wore glasses that provided me with perfect eyesight, but 20/20 vision without glasses was required for the navy program. As an alternative I hoped to get into the army R.O.T.C., whose entrance requirements were less rigid. I put in my application; but before it could be processed, I received my draft notice containing "Greetings" from the president. With only a semester of college before entering the army, my hopes of becoming an officer were slim.

Shortly before induction I was playing table tennis, and in a vigorous attempt to return the ball, I twisted my knee, forcing the cartilage out of place. I was unable to walk or straighten my leg, so I was taken to an osteopathic physician, who manipulated the cartilage to where it belonged. He applied an elastic band to support my knee because the cartilage might have become dislocated again if any strain occurred. I told the doctor that I was scheduled to go for military induction, and he gave me a note explaining that my knee's condition might be compromised if it were subject to unusual stress during military training. Also, if my leg were to malfunction during combat, my survival could be at risk.

With my knee in a brace and a note from the doctor, I went for the army physical examination.

When the army doctor saw the brace and asked me why I was wearing it, I told him the circumstances. I said that the cartilage would pop out of place under the slightest provocation when I squatted, because it had done so several times. When he asked whether I had a doctor's authentication of the injury, I showed him the note provided by the osteopath. When he saw that the note was from a physician other than an M.D., he declared it to be illegitimate. Then he told me to squat in an effort to force the cartilage out of place. I did so repeatedly and with vigor, but nothing happened. Despite the examiner's doubts about the veracity of my "trick" knee, he placed me on "Limited Service." This classification was used to designate a non-combat assignment.

The very next day I played in a recital at the conservatory in Philadelphia where I studied with the eminent French pianist, Emile Baume, and with Genia Robinor, an equally well-known Russian-born pianist. She played a command performance for the Queen of England, and performed at the White House for President Roosevelt. The pieces I played on that April 1st concert were Chopin's *"Great"* C Minor *Nocturne* and Prokofieff's *March* from the *Love of Three Oranges.*

One week after induction I was taken to Fort Dix reception center. There was no public transportation in our town, and a double-decker chartered bus took the recruits on a street where a bus had never been before. The street was lined on both sides by large shade trees such as sycamore, poplar, and Norway maple. The limbs from the trees formed an arch over the street; and they smashed every window on the upper deck on both sides of the bus. Flying glass wounded some of the recruits, and we had not yet seen military service!

My limited service status resulted in being assigned to a military police detachment at Fort Ontario, New York. Rather than the sixteen weeks of infantry basic training that I experienced later, our present training was rather mild. We were taught how to shoot, and police techniques used for crowd control, and for taking recalcitrant wrongdoers into custody.

Until this time, I had never fired a gun except for a few shots with a .22-caliber rifle owned by one of my boyhood friends. Many of the other men my age had been hunters in civilian life, and were familiar with powerful, large-caliber weapons. Some of the fellows, not wanting to be in the army, believed that they would be discharged from the service if they were unable to shoot well, and they deliberately fired all over the target, hoping to be sent home. Although I might have welcomed not going into the service so soon, so that I could finish my college education, I recognized and accepted the reality of our nation's need to fight for survival. For this reason, I was philosophical about being in the army, and felt a genuine sense of pride in being a soldier. Thus, I behaved myself, followed all the rules, and took in stride everything that was handed to me.

I admired the medals that other soldiers, who

were in the army for some time, wore on their uniforms, and I wanted medals of my own. I felt it to be somewhat demeaning to wear a "sharpshooter" or "marksman" medal, preferring instead the highest level designated as "expert." I paid attention to the details of how to shoot well: correct position, proper breath control, no flinching, precise sight picture, smooth trigger pull, follow-through, and whatever else necessary to hit the target precisely. Undoubtedly another important factor in shooting well is having the physical capability of holding the rifle steady. The upshot of all this is that I achieved the highest score in the entire battalion. We fired British Enfield rifles that were extremely accurate and reliable, but their recoil was unpleasant.

The rifle range at Fort Ontario, which was the oldest garrisoned fort in the United States, overlooked Lake Ontario. As the bullets pierced the targets they continued out into the lake, and we could see the splash in the water as the bullets hit. It was revealing to see so vividly how fast a missile actually was, traveling more than two thousand feet per second, from the time the trigger was pulled, until the bullet entered the water hundreds of yards distant!

Not long after our many all-day sessions on the firing range, I contracted naso-pharyngitis, a fancy name for a cold, and was sent to the hospital for several days. My company commander came to visit, and not wanting to be court-martialed for showing lack of respect, I sprang out of bed in my sick condition, and threw a snappy salute as he approached. He told me to get back into bed, and that I need not have saluted under those circumstances. He presented me with the expert rifleman's medal that I had recently earned because, being ill, I was absent from the awards ceremony. He began chatting with me about my previous shooting experience, assuming that I had been a hunter as a civilian. He found it to be incredulous when I told him that I had never before shot a high-powered rifle.

At the end of our training we were to be shipped to serve as MP's in New York City, Elmira, Binghamton, Syracuse, and Utica. Again I became ill, and went to the post hospital with the measles. All of the other men in the camp went to their assigned destinations, and I missed the shipment.

Chapter 14

Finance

After being released from the hospital, I was sent alone by train—there were only steam locomotives at that time—to Camp Kilmer in New Brunswick, New Jersey. The camp was named for Joyce Kilmer, author of the famous poem, *Trees*. He was killed in battle in Europe during the First World War.

Rather than being assigned to an MP outfit, for which I was trained, I was placed in a finance detachment in which virtually everyone had "limited service" classification. I, as already explained, had the knee that was subject to having the cartilage slip out of place. Some men wore thick glasses, and were they to lose them if they were in combat, there would be little hope of their surviving. One man was critically lame because one leg was shorter than the other, and his arm was carried as though it were in a sling. Another man had a bulging eye that was blind. One fellow, Joe O'Cain—I can't forget him—was over forty years old, and held a masters degree in economics. He was a real sot who staggered into the barrack every night after spending hours drinking beer in the post-exchange. He was loud and profane, and often threw up as a result of his overindulgence. I asked him why he bothered to come to the barrack, interrupting his binges at the PX. I suggested that he could save a lot of time by just lying at the bar and attaching a hose between the keg and his mouth. Another fellow, who was overly corpulent, wore glasses that were fastened to a chain attached to his shirt pocket button.

This group of misfits was assigned the duty of working on army payrolls. We computed wages of the base personnel, taking into account such considerations as rank, subsistence pay for dependents, and court-martial fines. It was, to be sure, easy and safe work. When the day's office duties ended, we changed from fatigues to dress uniforms appropriate for retiring the colors at retreat. The whole camp was present, and civilians from town came to see us march to music provided by the post band. Each unit was impressive looking as it passed in review in front of the camp commander. Our finance detachment, though, was an embarrassment, and I felt ashamed to be marching with this group of limping, glasses-on-a-chain, hunchbacked, wrinkled, withered arm, and staggering representatives of the armed forces.

After the evening meal, most of the camp personnel went to New Brunswick to the USO. It featured shows of various kinds, games, and dancing with the local girls. I always headed directly for the piano and played tunes that appealed to ordinary GI's, as well as classical compositions that I had studied and played in recitals as a civilian. While playing a particularly impressive and difficult piece one evening, I was joined by one of the girls—I'll just call her "Shirley"—who came regularly to dance and mingle with the soldiers from camp. She told me how well she thought I played, and said that she was also a pianist. We shared the spotlight playing for an enthusiastic group of listeners, and were approached by the USO club director who asked whether we would present a full-length program of piano music some weekend. I had no music with me, having no way to carry it or store it. Over the years—even though I was only eighteen at the time—I performed many times in public, and everything was played from memory; so I had in mental reserve many readily accessible piano works. In addition to our solo pieces we played duets by Brahms, Schubert, Mozart, and Moskowski. Shirley had an apartment above her parent's furniture store in the city, and she invited me to practice the duets where she lived.

Preparing the program required considerable time, and I had to be careful to leave in time to catch the bus back to camp. If I were late, and stranded until the next day, failure to appear at reveille the next morning would not be a good thing. After several evenings of practicing for the upcoming program, Shirley and I became comfortably acquainted. At the conclusion of one practice session, Shirley suggested that, rather than hurrying to catch the last bus for camp, I stay with her in the apartment and return to camp on an early morning bus. For some reason or another, people to whom I tell this incident feel that my response to her invitation was somewhat odd. I said, "That's very kind of you, but I think it would be more ethical if I were to get back to camp tonight."

Chapter 15
Subway Commandos

I was at Camp Kilmer for only a couple of months when a notice was distributed announcing the formation of the Army Specialized Training Program, or ASTP. It was designed to train men to become officers in the Corps of Engineers, and those who qualified would be sent to any of a number of colleges and universities throughout the country to take an accelerated curriculum in basic engineering. After pursuing specialization as a mechanical, chemical, or electrical engineer, the candidate would receive his commission.

This appealed to me from the moment I first heard about it; but strangely, quite a few men were suspicious of going into anything for which they might be invited to volunteer. Old Joe O'Cain, my drunken colleague mentioned earlier, told me to jump at the opportunity, wisely counseling me on the benefits of a good education, and especially of becoming an officer. Some of my buddies, however, opted out, not wanting to risk giving up the safe and easy duties of working in finance, or the presumed permanence of location where one would not be sent overseas as a combatant.

I took O'Cain's advice, passed the entrance examinations, and was on my way to Manhattan's

City College of New York. Because of Joe's age—
he certainly was smart enough—he himself was
not qualified to enter the program. As I was shak-
ing hands with him, about to depart for New York,
he said to me, "Let me give you one last word: as
you undertake this schooling, always do your own
work. Never let anyone do the work for you." This
was a gentle and euphemistic way of telling me not
to cheat.

College life at CCNY was wonderful beyond
description. We knew that we were still in the army,
with its "spit and polish," military discipline, and
physical conditioning. Rather than running cross-
country up and down hills, and groveling in the dirt
as troops in training do routinely, we kept in shape
with activities found on campus, virtually in the
heart of Manhattan. There were the ever-present
daily calisthenics, but several hours each day were
spent with gymnasium equipment, or running, wrestling, boxing, fencing, swimming, water polo, bas-
ketball, touch football, and rifle shooting. Everyone
was exposed to all of the above, but we could devote
more time to our preferences if we chose. I never was
very good at team sports, but did well in wrestling
and fencing.

All of our sports and academic instructors were
civilians, and many of them held earned doctorates.
They always addressed us as "Private So-and-So,"
and we always responded with "Sir," as we would if
we were addressing army officers.

Our academic studies were intensive, and there

were no free periods from early morning until ten o'clock at night (2200 hours). Everybody took the same pre-engineering courses: mathematics (algebra, solid analytical geometry, calculus), chemistry (physical and organic), physics (mechanics, heat, light, sound, electricity, etc.), laboratory classes in the sciences, mechanical drawing, history, literature, and public speaking, to name a few. There was no letup from the academic classes or the physical education activities except during meals. After supper we marched to a huge study hall to do homework; and there was no fooling around.

The prime incentive for getting good grades was the realistic threat of being removed from ASTP and being sent to a combat unit destined for overseas duty. I remember specifically one of the men in a mathematics class who failed one of the tests, and realized the consequences. He pleaded with the professor, saying, "But Dr. Mallon, if you flunk me, I'll be sent to combat!"

The professor responded kindly, but matter-of-factly, "Well, that's life!" We all groaned sympathetically.

The professors were outstanding, fully-qualified people, but the laboratory assistants were sometimes incompetent. This became evident in a chemistry lab when the assistant was showing us crystals of the element iodine in a test tube. We knew that iodine sublimes; that is, when heat is applied, it changes from a solid to a vapor, and does not liquefy, as do most substances. As we viewed the contents of the test tube, we saw drops of moisture with the iodine crystals. "Well, what do you know about that?" remarked the assistant. "Liquid iodine!" Students who were close to the test tube noticed that the liquid was clear, and not the same reddish-purple color as iodine. The assistant suddenly remembered that he had just washed out the test tube, and didn't dry it. Such ignorance!

In physics lab an assistant was attempting to show the effects of an intense heat source located at the focal point of a parabolic mirror, having its heat transferred by reflection via parallel rays across the room to another parabolic mirror, the rays converging to the focal point of this mirror. A stunning phenomenon is accomplished by having a carbon arc located at the first mirror's focal point, and a two-by-four block of wood supported at the focal point of the second mirror some distance away. When done correctly, the awesomely hot flame from the carbon arc is dispersed to impotence as it traverses the distance between the two mirrors; but when the rays converge at the focus of the second mirror, the block of wood immediately catches fire. The experiment was a flop when the assistant merely turned on the switch, sending an electric current to the carbon electrodes, expecting them to ignite. Nothing happened, of course. He called in the professor to ascertain why there was no flame, and the professor simply struck the two carbon electrodes together, closing the circuit, and then as they were pulled apart, the flame occurred as expected. With the professor's knowledgeable intervention, the spectacle was a success.

One other lab experiment gone awry was intended to show a physics truism that any object in motion, having no force acting on it, must of necessity slow down until it stops, and can never, by itself, accelerate. To prove this, a heavy solid metal ball about eight inches in diameter was suspended on a rope from a high ceiling in the lecture hall. The ball rested, hanging on the rope, a few inches above the floor. The professor took the hanging ball in his hands, and, allowing the rope to remain taut, backed up, holding the ball until it barely touched the professor's nose. Standing absolutely still, he released the ball, permitting it to swing like a pendulum through its full arc, and then letting it return. Although it appears scary, there is no danger of the ball's ever reaching its initial point of release; therefore the professor's nose escaped impact with the ball.

The lab assistant observed the professor conduct the experiment, and was told to show the next class the identical procedure. He followed each phase of the process exactly as demonstrated, until it was time to release the ball. Rather than merely letting go of it, however, he *pushed* it! There was a big surprise when the ball's return swing went farther than where it was released.

At ten o'clock at night we marched back to the barrack, and could do whatever we wanted for another hour or so until lights out. My closest friend, Bill Banister (with whom I continue to correspond), and I usually strolled down Amsterdam Avenue to a

Jewish delicatessen for a bedtime snack. My usual choice of food was a quart of buttermilk and an entire pound cake. Despite this high caloric intake plus our exceptionally adequate and nutritious meals provided in the dining hall, I weighed one hundred eighty pounds, was five feet eleven and a half inches tall, and had a thirty-three inch waist.

Privileges such as weekend passes would be withdrawn for infringement of the rules. When taps was sounded everyone was expected to be in bed. Not surprisingly, there were always those who did not follow regulations, and the officer-of-the-day or perhaps the company commander would conduct nightly bed check. The lights were off in each barrack, and the inspecting officer walked through in the dark, using his flashlight to shine randomly at the bunks to see whether anyone was absent. The inspection customarily happened a couple of hours after taps, and those who were in bed asleep did not take too kindly to having a light shining in their faces.

A way was found to discourage such encroachment. We tied ropes across the aisles a few inches from the floor, attached to legs of the bunks. This simple process had its intended effect of causing the inspector to stumble, and fall to the floor. His muttered invectives elicited muffled chortling from the men in their bunks. Astonishingly, no retribution was inflicted for this potentially serious offence, likely because no one could be directly blamed. Because the ropes were tied to somebody's bed did not necessarily mean that the person in that bed attached the ropes; anyone could have done it.

A case of blaming someone else for something he did not do occurred when we had barrack inspection. We were required to hang certain articles of clothing in a prescribed order, and items such as underwear, socks, razor, comb, and the like had to be aligned in the footlocker at the end of the bunk precisely as specified. Everything that might accumulate dust was to be cleaned; shoes had to be exactly in alignment, and the floor under and surrounding the bunk had to be mopped.

I dutifully followed all of the requirements, but for some reason or another, did not mop up the dust under my bunk. After inspection I found my name on the company bulletin board showing a demerit for the dirty floor. I went to the orderly room and asked permission to see the company commander. He was a "ninety day wonder," the term of scorn chosen to describe young second lieutenants who received their commissions after a mere three months of OCS (Officer Candidate School). He was an unimpressive, short, pipsqueak who, when he saluted, tilted his head down to meet his hand rather than bring his hand up sharply to his brow; and he walked with a sort of hopping gait that led us to refer to him as "the rabbit."

I entered his office, saluted him, and indignantly asserted that I, indeed, cleaned under my bunk. The windows of the barrack were open, and I averred that the dust must have been blown by the wind from the man's bunk next to mine. As I think about this, even today, I must admit that it sounds like a weak argument. It convinced the lieutenant, however. He removed the demerit and I received my weekend pass!

It would be difficult to imagine a better circumstance under which to live as a soldier than in an ASTP unit, especially in New York City, an ideal location where one could enjoy weekend passes. During the nine months that I was stationed at City College, I took the equivalent of two years of engineering courses that served as transfer credits towards my Bachelor of Science degree when I returned to civilian life.

There was resentment against us soldiers on the part of the civilians who lived in the tenements in the area near the college. They recognized, of course, that we were living the "life of Riley" in our safe environment, while many of them had loved ones who were fighting overseas; and we were also fully aware and appreciative of our good fortune. As we marched from the barrack to classes down Amsterdam Avenue or other streets in the area, we were sometimes met with jeers, being labeled "subway commandos." We took such umbrage in stride, recognizing that we were assigned to be here, and were preparing to become officers for important and legitimate roles designed to win the war.

When the school week came to a close on Friday evenings, almost everybody headed for the subway station to take the train for glorious fun on Times Square. I sometimes went with one or more soldier friends to the Stage Door Canteen, the setting for a movie in 1943. The actual establishment was rather seedy, compared to the allure with which it was garbed by Hollywood. Another popular attraction was the USO sponsored by Pepsi Cola. It featured hostesses, games, and all the free Pepsi we could drink. It also had a grand piano at which I often presided, and I always garnered an appreciative crowd. Broadway shows and famous big bands led by Xavier Cugat, Duke Ellington, Count Basie, and the like were popular; and soldiers in uniform were admitted free of charge.

Virtually everyone in the civilized world was aware of the New Year's celebration that occurred annually in Times Square, and I looked forward to being there in person to bid farewell to 1943 and to welcome 1944. I went with my friend Bill Banister to the intersection of Broadway and 42nd Street a few hours before midnight, and the streets were already crowded to overflowing with revelers. Most able-bodied men there were in uniform; there were not many civilian men present, and women without escorts were in profusion.

Bill and I separated, his having seen a girl who seemed willing to be his date for the evening's Times Square festivities. I had a girlfriend home in New Jersey, and had no interest in being with a stranger at that time. I saw many drunken people, prematurely celebrating the ringing in of the New Year, and was disinclined to "let myself go" in these festivities. I was still only nineteen years old, and never drank alcohol.

Around eleven o'clock I took the subway train back to CCNY. When I arrived at the barrack, I saw only one other person at the far end. He didn't see me, as far as I knew, and neither of us made an effort to say anything.

My home was about ninety miles south of New York, and some weekends I would go home to visit my parents and my girlfriend, rather than go downtown to Times Square. The electric train could take me to Philadelphia in about an hour and a half, and I would board a bus or a commuter train to cross the Delaware River, and then take another bus to my house. This was too much of a hassle to make the round trip home every free weekend.

There is an old adage that states, "All good things come to an end." This proverbial truism became evident when the war required more combat personnel, and resulted in disbanding the ASTP programs throughout the United States.

Chapter 16

Missed Chances

There was a well-known cartoon character at the time known as the "Sad Sack." He was a pitiable soldier who was constantly beset by every imaginable misfortune. When we received word that our college careers were to end, every one of us instantly thought of himself as the ultimate Sad Sack. We learned that many air force cadets, too, who hoped to become pilots, bombardiers, and navigators, were destined to fill more lowly positions.

Wait! There was yet hope. Although ASTP had ceased, there was an opportunity to apply for medical school. No one knew how long the war would last, and there was a desperate need for physicians. When I was hospitalized as a thirteen year old with appendicitis and pleural pneumonia, I so admired the doctors that I wanted to become one. One of the prime reasons I decided against it was that my doctor, hearing that I played the piano, wanted to hear me play when he visited our house. (In those days, almost all doctors made house calls.) After listening to me play, he was impressed enough to advise me to stay with music and forget about going into medicine. If he had my talent, he declared that he would have been a musician instead of a physician!

With this early predilection for being a physician, I eagerly anticipated being chosen for the medical training that was being made available. To qualify, candidates were required to take a battery of tests to determine aptitude for becoming a doctor. As preparation for the tests, we were given lists of medical terminology and diagrams relating to the human anatomy, and were asked to learn the names and functions of bones, organs, nerves, and similar categories. This posed no difficulty for me, and I successfully completed the examinations. The next step for being accepted to the program was an interview with an army doctor. I recall his telling me that I passed the preliminary weeding-out process, and he wanted me to explain how devoted I would be to pursuing the lengthy and arduous pursuit of a medical degree. I thought that I stated my willingness to do so convincingly, but the examiner noted music as my major upon entering college as a civilian. I assured him that I had many interests and aptitudes, and that I could be successful in any number of careers. I called to his attention my excellent grades in the engineering curriculum in ASTP that attested to that fact. He persisted in reminding me that my first preference must necessarily have been music, otherwise I would not have chosen it as my college major. He had me in the proverbial "bind," and I was unable to break the impasse. I was turned down, and knew of no viable alternative but to join my disheartened ASTP buddies in whatever lay ahead.

Before leaving for our unknown destiny, we were given new physical examinations. It was night-time, and as irrational as it may sound, we were ushered into an unlit room where we were checked to see whether our selective service classification should be altered. The doctor looked down my throat, listened to my heart, and announced to an assistant with a list of our names that I was 1-A, the top designation that qualifies a recruit for combat duty. Someone told me later—and I don't know how true it is—that reclassification after induction was unlawful. True or not, my future rested on the results of an evaluation in a dark room.

Chapter 17
This is It!

None of us had any inkling of what our next assignment would be when we were herded onto a troop train at Grand Central Station. Having had our recent college study, many such as myself whose classification was overturned, doubted that we would be placed in a branch of service befitting our education. After we boarded, an officer told us that our orders would be forthcoming after we left the station. There was universal concern about keeping troop movements secret.

Rumors were rampant concerning our future. No one informed us where we were traveling, but we observed signs along the route that indicated we were still in the state of New York for the first few hours. For the first night, the train was parked on a railroad bridge near Niagara Falls. For the next four days we noticed that we were in Michigan, Illinois, Indiana, Missouri, Arkansas, Mississippi, and Louisiana. Though we were on a troop train, we rode in Pullman cars and slept in upper and lower berths. This was a new experience for me, and I vowed that I would travel extensively by rail when I became a civilian after the war. We spent our time watching the scenery and playing cards. I was introduced to bridge for the first time. It seemed too bothersome to be fun, and I never played bridge again until ten years later. It is now one of my most ardent pastimes.

After several days en route, the officer in charge announced in a dramatic manner that we were being sent to—we all held our breath—the 75th Infantry Division! Horror of horrors! We were truly sad sacks beyond reprieve. In an attempt to assuage our fears and disappointment, the officer stated exultantly that we were to be in the "Queen of Battle!" As time went on, I had to agree with this assessment; for although the training as well as real combat were often onerous and filled with dread, I felt a deep pride in belonging to what was, to me, an elite branch of service.

After five days and nights on the train we arrived after dark in Shreveport, Louisiana. We boarded two-and-a-half-ton army trucks and were transported to Camp Polk. I looked forward to a good meal and a bed; but it was not to be. We were issued two large barracks bags to be designated as "A" bag and "B" bag. We were given new uniforms, OD's (olive drabs) and fatigues (non-dress work clothes), back pack, M-1 Garand rifle, bayonet, steel helmet and liner, cartridge belt, medical pouch, shelter half (part of a tent which could be attached to another soldier's half to form a complete tent), tent pegs and ropes, underwear, socks, handkerchiefs, ammunition, mess gear (dish and lid, cup, utensils), canteen and cover, shirts and ties, toilet articles, two pairs of boots, raincoat, blanket, folding shovel, and several cans of food rations.

All of this equipment was literally "thrown" at

us, and orders were barked at us, designating which items were to go into bag "A" and which were to go into bag "B." I was still in a state of shock to find myself in this most unlikely plight imaginable, and so tired because it was after midnight, and having to sort out the issued items into their respective bags, that I didn't know for certain which bag was which. The bags were identified by our last initial and the last four numbers of our army serial number, and taken away by truck. Mine were marked B-6018. We kept only essential items that we could carry on our backs or belts, enough for surviving outdoors for a month of simulated combat maneuvers.

By this time it was the middle of the night, and we were given a full supper consisting of meat loaf, potatoes, vegetables, bread, pudding, and coffee. We were put on trucks and taken through dense woods having narrow, unpaved lanes rather than roads. After what seemed to be a couple of hours, we joined members of the division who were in the midst of maneuvers, already having had sixteen weeks of infantry basic training. They were already seasoned soldiers, and when they learned that we had not undergone the rigors of being in the infantry, but were college students who had lived in Manhattan, they treated us shamefully.

When we arrived at the bivouac area, it was pouring rain and miserably cold. We had no idea about how to make a tent out of the shelter halves, and because it was dark, we could not see any place to lie down to sleep. The men who were already there paid no attention to us, and we stood up all night, leaning against trees because we didn't want to lie down in puddles or in the mud.

When daylight came we were assigned to our respective units. I was classified as a rifleman and assigned to "B" Company, 3rd Battalion, and 289th Regiment. We marched many miles every day, following orders as required in the war games. It was late in the spring; the days were hot and the nights were uncomfortably cold. My longest day's march was thirty miles, and it rained heavily for much of the time. We walked through cotton fields, woods, open areas, and swamps. Other military units had been there before us, and dug countless foxholes, which were usually seven feet deep with a step one foot high; but they did not fill them up again when they left the area. Several times, as I waded through water up to my knees, or even waist deep, I stepped into a foxhole and disappeared from sight. I would thrust my rifle up over my head, and a companion would grab it and pull me to the surface. Many times we crossed streams by walking across fallen logs that stretched from one bank to the other. They were wet and slippery, and I often fell from the log into the water.

While on the march we ate canned "C" rations and baloney or cheese sandwiches made with thick slices of army-baked white bread. We filled our canteens with water from streams, and made it safe for drinking by adding tablets containing chlorine. The pills made the water taste bad, and the water taken directly from the streams was made further unpalatable because it was discolored, sometimes containing green slime and insects. When we were in bivouac, water was dispensed in canvas Lister bags. It, too, was treated with chlorine and tasted terrible, but at least it was clean.

There were times when an absurd order was given, forbidding us from drinking any water for extended periods. This was intended to inure us for surviving in the event of an actual unforeseen water shortage. After one particularly strenuous march that made me extremely thirsty, I stated that I would be willing to give a full month's wages for one bottle of Coca-Cola, and I meant it!

We constantly changed locations, engaging in mock battles between our "blue" army and the "red" army, who were the "enemy." Sometimes we were in Louisiana, or we would cross the Sabine River into Texas. I crossed once in a rubber raft, a couple of times on a pontoon bridge, and on a rope bridge. This latter device consisted of three parallel ropes strung from one bank of the river to the other. We walked on a bottom strand while holding the other two strands, which served as handrails.

For distances too far to march, we were transported in two-and-a-half-ton trucks. It was astonishing that we could ride—"bounce" would be a more descriptive term—for hour after hour without seeing even one road in either Texas or Louisiana. I had come to believe that neither state had any paved roads.

When we settled down to camp for the night, we would have welcomed a fire to create a bit of warmth. However, at those times when we were engaged in a war game scenario, we dared not expose our position; so having even a small fire was prohibited. When a "battle" episode was completed, and fires were permitted, I stood for such extended periods in front of the fire, both day and night, that my face and hands became covered with thick, crusty scabs, the result of my flesh being scorched.

When we slept at night, we never removed any of our clothing or our boots. If we were required to leave the area in a hurry in darkness, it was necessary to be ready in an instant; and if our leather boots were wet—as they often were—they would shrink and become misshapen so that we could not put them on quickly.

"Live" ammunition was rarely used during maneuvers, and there were few accidental injuries caused by our weapons. There were a few fatalities, however. One resulted from a truck's running over a sleeping man, and another man died from a rattlesnake bite. Yet another drowned when the raft in which he was riding capsized while crossing the Sabine River.

We were advised to inspect the insides of our boots before putting them on, to make certain they were empty of snakes or scorpions. Harmless armadillos and collared peccaries were everywhere.

Periodically, there were kitchen trucks in our area, and it was a treat to eat something other than canned or boxed cold rations. About two or three o'clock one morning, we were awakened and told to report to the kitchen truck for an early breakfast. Most of the men would have preferred to remain asleep rather than go to breakfast, but we were told, "Every man will eat!" It was pitch dark, and I had no idea where the kitchen truck was located. Everyone was stumbling around, carrying his mess gear, and tripping over fallen tree branches, gullies, and various protuberances on the ground. I finally found the truck and was given a full, heavy, meal—whether it was a late supper or early breakfast, I do not know— consisting of meat, vegetables, bread, dessert, etc., but I was in no mood to eat very much at this hour. As was the practice when the meal was finished, we sloshed our mess kits in hot soapy water, wiped them with a dish mop, and dunked them in scalding rinse water. I headed back to my company, but there were no bearings that enabled me to locate where I was to go. Groping in the blackness, I would bump into somebody and ask, "Is this "B" Company? Who is this?"

No one gave me an affirmative answer, and I didn't recognize any of the names. I continued my inquiry, thumping various soldiers on the arm and asking who they were, but I still didn't know anyone. After several such encounters, one of the people whom I whacked in the arm told me his name, but it was unfamiliar to me. He then asked me, "Who are you?"

Realizing that he was not a member of my company, I said, "Oh, you wouldn't know me, anyhow." Immediately a flashlight was shined in my face, and at an officer wearing a silver bar on his collar.

A voice coming from a second officer bellowed, "Didn't you hear him say he was Lieutenant Van Raleigh?" I assured him that I did not hear his identifying himself, then both officers berated me for not showing proper recognition and respect for superior rank. They said that there was going to be real discipline in this outfit, and that I would be subject to being court-martialed. I endeavored to convince them that what I did was done innocently, and meant no disrespect. Finally, they calmed down, directed me to my company, and nothing further came of the incident.

It was obvious to my platoon sergeant that we newcomers, unaccustomed to the rigors of outdoor army life, were unhappy and felt miserable. The sergeant bragged that he volunteered for the infantry, and I replied that he must be dumber than he looked. Subsequently, I had only myself to blame when I was assigned more frequently than anyone else such work details as digging garbage disposal pits four feet deep and four feet square, digging slit trench latrines, or scrubbing grease, grime, and rust from cook stoves, using sandpaper and a wire brush.

It is evident that I was being selected arbitrarily for the dirty tasks, and I had the temerity to tell the sergeant that I was being unfairly discriminated against when these jobs were assigned. He told me that he would correct the situation by making a duty roster, thereby distributing the workload more equitably. He listed the names alphabetically, and my name, beginning with "B," was first on each day's roster. My situation did not improve; it became worse!

My naiveté and lack of judgment became evident when the sergeant wanted me to give him my canned rations. He had already eaten his, and had only the bologna and cheese sandwiches which each of us had received earlier from the kitchen truck. He decided that he and I would roll dice, and if my roll were lower than his, I would give him my rations. If my roll were higher than his, I would not have to dig the next sixty-four cubic foot garbage pit. I rolled first, and threw "snake eyes." The sergeant did not roll, but declaring that he was the winner, took my rations! What if he also rolled a "two?" Would there be a re-roll? Could it be that his dice were loaded?

Being outranked and intimidated by his customary attitude towards me, I was reluctant to seek recourse. The other men who witnessed this travesty of fairness sympathized with me in private. They recognized his flawed character, but were also afraid to say anything. Someone, however, must have called the sergeant's crass behavior to the attention of the officers, because not too long afterward he was demoted and transferred to another unit.

Chapter 18

Civilization

I longed for the time when we would be living again in a barrack, so that we could be warm and dry, take a shower, drink clean water, wear clean clothes, and eat cooked food while sitting at a table. My friend, Bill Banister, whom I mentioned earlier, spoke more disparagingly about being in the military than I did. He had nothing positive to say, even though his grandfather had been a colonel in the medical corps, or some other enviable position whose details I don't clearly recall. On one occasion we were standing in line in the pouring rain, waiting to have our mess kits filled. As we passed from one kettle of food to the next, each kitchen police (KP) server dumped the portions on top of the other food items, so that everything, main dish, dessert—no matter what—was mixed together. The mélange of helpings looked even more unappetizing, because the rainstorm soaked everything. I said to Bill, "Do you realize that the only thing a GI lives for is a weekend pass and chow?"

Viewing the undistinguishable agglomeration in his mess kit, he retorted with a sneer, "And what chow!" Not only were passes unavailable while on maneuvers, but the one remaining thing for which a GI lived, namely chow, was not worth having.

Finally, after the month-long ordeal under the open sky, maneuvers came to an end, and we were on our way by train to the eagerly anticipated, comparative luxury of living indoors. Our destination was Camp Breckinridge, Kentucky, located within a short distance from Evansville, Indiana.

During the entire time I was on maneuvers, being often cold and wet, I never had so much as a sniffle. Within twenty-four hours of living in a barrack, I and many other soldiers acquired hacking coughs and sore throats.

Most of the men whom we joined on maneuvers, and who came with us now to Breckinridge, were issued new equipment immediately, and sent overseas. They, unlike us, had already had infantry training at Fort Leonard Wood. Now we had to undergo the rigor of sixteen weeks of training for combat. We attended daily classes in military tactics, fired rifles and carbines, went on endurance marches, threw hand grenades, engaged in bayonet practice, ran the obstacle course, learned how to recognize poison gasses and use our gasmasks, practiced stealth in order to kill sentries, engaged in hand-to-hand combat, and as the culminating task to verify our readiness for combat, went through the infiltration course. This was an exercise in which we crawled on our stomachs under barbed wire as bombs were detonated alongside us, and live machinegun ammunition was fired over our heads three feet above the ground.

What could have had a devastating consequence occurred when we were taught to throw live hand grenades. We practiced with dummy grenades, pulling the safety pin, and strived for accuracy by tossing them through wooden frames designed to resemble open windows. When it was time to throw the real thing, we had been through the ritual of pulling the pin and getting rid of the grenade so many times, that the procedure became automatic, and we were comfortable doing it.

On the day we were to use real grenades, a cook who had no combat training, joined us. He was assigned to the kitchen and excused from normal training because he was missing a forefinger, the "trigger" finger. Because he was not exposed to combat training, nor had experience with dummy grenades, he was almost in a state of apoplexy with fright. We were standing alongside each other behind a mound of earth, to protect us from the shrapnel of the exploding grenade after it was thrown over an embankment. Only one man at a time threw his grenade. As each of us stepped, in turn, up to the barrier of earth, we were given the command to "Pull pin!" then we were told to toss the grenade, and stoop down to avoid the blast. Everyone followed directions, and his grenade detonated safely on the other side of the earthen barricade. When it was the cook's turn, and given the order to pull the pin, he froze, and cried, "I can't do it! I can't do it!"

The rest of us were alongside him, crouching down so as to avoid being killed by the blast of his grenade after it was thrown. He just stood there, petrified, and we had no idea whether he would pull the pin, drop the grenade, throw it, or run away. A lieutenant was in charge, and he calmly talked to the cook, telling him to take it easy, and not to pull the safety pin. The officer slowly and patiently reviewed the procedures with him as we crouched down, not knowing the outcome of this potential catastrophe. The officer's authoritative and assuring manner enabled the agitated, flustered cook finally to discharge the grenade without incident.

Inspections of one kind or another are universal in the military; at least I found it to be so in every outfit to which I was ever assigned. Incentive for complying with the regulations was great, because failing to do so resulted most often in being deprived of a "pass" to leave the base. While in formation the soldier is examined from head to toe: uniform spotless, shoes shined to a high gloss, tie neatly knotted, buttons fastened, cap at proper angle, close shave, and weapon spotless. When preparing for guard duty in our company, the soldier who most impeccably met the inspection standards was issued a three-day pass. I always fulfilled requirements, but never earned the bonus because I didn't go the "extra mile," so to speak. Our clothes were cleaned at the post laundry, but they were not pressed fastidiously. Typically, the soldiers who met the highest inspection standards ironed their shirts—or paid someone to do it—with so-called "military" creases in front and back. It sounds like a joke that some men ironed their shoelaces in pursuit of the coveted pass, but it isn't.

Specific inspection requirements varied, depending on where we were located. In one camp where it was hot and humid, our rifles were given a light coat of oil after being cleaned. At another camp that was dry and dusty, all oil was to be removed. Regulations varied among bases regarding the order in which clothing was to be arranged when hung up, or how items were displayed in footlockers at the ends of the cots. I once received demerits when the inspecting officer found a fleck of lint in the slot of the screw that attached the handle to my bayonet. I couldn't see the speck when I examined the slot. Did it fall out? Was it a figment in the imagination of an overzealous officer? It seemed an unfair justification for being deprived of a weekend pass, but whoever claimed that the army was fair?

Upon completion of training, and about to leave for a port of embarkation, I became sick, and was sent to the post hospital. While I was recovering, my fellow soldiers with whom I had trained, left Breckinridge, and I remained behind. Meanwhile, a group of new recruits came into the camp, and I was assigned to their unit to undergo my second stint of sixteen weeks of infantry basic training!

As it turned out, the additional time spent was not a complete loss. I was transferred from being a rifleman to being a member of a machinegun platoon. As a kid I never knew how a machinegun operated, and was eager to fire one. When I was still a rifleman I was trained to fire the type of machinegun that had a shoulder stock and rested on a bipod as the shooter lay on the ground. The ammunition belt contained one tracer bullet for every three non-tracers. We fired on what was called a transitional range, at pop-up silhouette targets from two to six hundred yards distant.

The machinegun to which I was now assigned in my new platoon was a major weapon in an infantry arsenal, and required a three-man team to operate it. One man carried the gun, one carried the tripod needed to support the gun and provide elevating and transitional axes for aiming, and the third man carried the ammunition. The machinegun squad was a close comradeship, and Platoon Sergeant McGraw was a patient and sympathetic leader whose manner elicited our loyalty and respect.

Being a machine gunner was more exciting than being a rifleman, but the hazards of serving in this capacity on the battlefield were obvious, his being a prime target for the enemy. When I wrote to my parents about my new assignment they were distraught, understandably, and my mother became hysterical. Her dilemma and my role in the army would soon change, however.

Chapter 19
A Different Weapon

It was my custom to attend the post chapel for Sunday services and to meet with a small group of my fellow soldiers for midweek Bible study. In addition to a Roman Catholic chaplain were two Protestant chaplains, one Methodist and one Baptist, and I became well acquainted with all three of them. On Sunday evenings our Bible study group would conduct worship services at churches (at their invitation) in various towns neighboring Camp Breckinridge. One soldier would preach the sermon, others would lead the Scripture readings, and I played the organ for the prelude, offering, and hymn-singing.

Before entering the army I practiced the piano several hours every day, which was required for maintaining skill in pursuing a professional career in music. Now I was no longer able to keep up this regimen, but I used every available opportunity to play pianos in company dayrooms and at USO (United Service Organization) centers when I went into town on pass at the end of the day.

An official from one of the radio stations in Evansville, Indiana was at the USO center, and after hearing me play some classical piano pieces, invited me to play a live broadcast at his radio studio. I still remember that, among the compositions I performed, were Chopin's *Polonaise in C Minor* and Brahms' *"Edward" Ballade.*

I never liked electronic organs, but they were the prevailing instruments in army chapels throughout the country. I requested permission to practice on the chapel organ during free time, and Chaplain Prentis, the Methodist chaplain, granted it. He needed someone to replace his assistant who was forty years old, and was to receive early discharge because of family hardship.

There was a candidate to fill the position, but he was not a musician. Ideally, the chaplain's assistant should be qualified to play the organ for services, to drive a jeep, to serve as a secretary, and function essentially as a sort of aide-de-camp. It was relatively easy to find an assistant who could fill most of these duties, but the ability most difficult to find in a candidate was that of playing the organ.

I was able to type rapidly, although I used the "hunt-and-peck" method. When I was seventeen years old, the legal age for driving a car in New Jersey, I did not acquire a license, realizing that my civilian days were soon coming to a close. Chaplain Prentis felt that my secretarial and driving skills could be readily polished, and recognizing that my musical background was more than expected, asked me to work for him.

Contrary to what many people would assume, a combat chaplain's duty could be genuinely hazardous. There were documented cases of more than a few chaplains losing their lives in war. It stands to reason, however, that a chaplain's assistant's survival would be significantly greater than that of serving in a machinegun platoon. Despite perilous encounters with the enemy, which will be described later, I received only an insignificant wound; but every one of the men in my former machinegun platoon were either killed or severely injured.

The skill that I needed most to acquire in a hurry was that of driving the chaplain's jeep. I knew the essentials of how to operate a car, but a jeep had its own peculiarities. There were no automatic transmissions in the military vehicles of the 1940's, and jeeps had three gearshifts. One supplied the front wheels with power, one was a standard three-speed and reverse lever, and the third engaged a transfer case that provided low-gear power for extreme terrain or load requirements. Prentis' assistant who was soon to leave the service took me in the boondocks where there were no roads, but only steep hills, gullies, ditches, rocks, gravel, and almost any other impediment to driving that one could imagine. It wasn't long before I was able to negotiate any terrain that the jeep was designed to accommodate.

Author as chaplain's assistant.
(Notice cross beneath windshield on right of jeep.)

All of the vehicles in our division had names painted on them for identification, and a particular letter of the alphabet designated each battalion. Our battalion's jeeps and trucks had names beginning with the letter "L," so it was appropriate that the Protestant chaplains' jeeps were named *Luke* and *Leviticus*. I no longer remember the name of the Catholic chaplain's jeep, but I hardly believe it was *Lamentations*, the only other book of the Bible beginning with "L." My mother wanted me to have my jeep painted with her name, *Laura,* but I told her that I was not authorized to change the name. *Leviticus* was manufactured by Ford, and was a rough-riding vehicle. *Luke* was made by Willys, and had a wonderfully soft ride. If both vehicles were available, Chaplain Prentis would always tell me to take *Luke*.

I hardly became acquainted with my duties

under Prentis, when a new chaplain, James P. Morgan, arrived. He had the rank of captain, and became the head chaplain for the battalion, and he chose me as his assistant, with Prentis having a new, less experienced person take my place.

As the chaplain's assistant, rather than being in a machine gun squad, I felt virtually no apprehension about going overseas. My chief worry, however, continued to be my mother's mental state, realizing how protective she had always been, and that she could do nothing but fret about my welfare. The troops were given a final furlough, and I went by train for a last visit with my parents and my girlfriend. Even though my CA duties reduced the potential for being killed or maimed, my mother's anxiety was not quelled. I learned after returning from the war that she ranted hysterically, and heard me calling to her in distress at night.

Returning again to camp, all was in readiness for an overseas destiny. We boarded a train, arriving in Camp Shanks, the embarkation center near New York City. It seemed reasonable that we were going to Europe, because a Pacific theater assignment would more than likely take us to a west coast port. There continued to be rumors suggesting that Asia might be our destiny, but the matter was settled when we were shown how to search an enemy soldier for weapons, and the people assuming the role of the enemy were attired in German uniforms. Biding our time for the few days until we boarded ship, our only last-minute training was climbing rope ladders that hung from the side of a vessel for transferring to a smaller boat.

Finally our day of departure arrived, and a few members of our regimental service company, to which I belonged, were assigned as an advanced party to a cabin on the converted British luxury liner, H.M.T. (Her Majesty's Transport) *Franconia.* Everyone else, except the officers—which included a group of army nurses—slept on hammocks in multiple tiers on the lower decks. I felt sorry for those in their cramped quarters, and "I" Company suffered the worst indignity by having permanent KP for the entire voyage.

There were about ten of us in our cabin, and I remember specifically the Catholic chaplain's assistant, "Spike" Moynihan. "Spike," whose true name I didn't know, had boxed professionally before entering the service. He was a good-natured fellow, and I was sure that I would not be injured when he volunteered to show me some moves that are a part of the sport of boxing. I had done a little boxing in physical education class at CCNY, and did well enough because my opponents were no more skilled than I was. I "put up my dukes" against "Spike," and it required no more than a nanosecond for him to land a punch to my jaw. It was all in fun, so he didn't hit me very hard. Although I held up my fists to protect myself, "Spike" was able to feint so skillfully, that I dropped my guard and was unable to ward off his blow. This showed me firsthand that an adversary with real boxing skills has the edge against someone who is larger in height and weight, but lacks the finesse of a trained fighter.

Also in our cabin was a recreational director whose name I don't recall, but whose stage name was Rodney Colbin when he worked as an actor in civilian life. Another cabin mate was a semi-professional baseball player before entering the service. He constantly tried to elevate his professional status by saying that every member of the baseball team is of equal importance, and that my performing in concerts on a stage was no more important than the stagehands that adjust the lighting and pull the curtain; or the ushers, the ticket taker, or the janitor who cleans the auditorium. All deserved equal pay, and required as much skill!

Our convoy was said to be one of the biggest ever to cross the Atlantic during the war. The portholes of our ship were painted so that the inside lights would not give away our presence to German submarines. There were rough seas with fifty-foot high waves during much of our eleven-day crossing. I became woozy, but was not seriously seasick; so in an effort to feel better, I went frequently on deck for fresh air. There were ropes strung along the deck as handholds to keep one from falling down or being washed overboard. Our ship was escorted by navy cruisers and destroyers, and I was fascinated by watching their prows dipping into the sea, completely submerged, as they made their way through the storms. At night I saw the luminescent froth stirred up by the ship's wake and the propellers at the stern. I saw too, as I had heard somewhere, that the

Gulf Stream is a different color from the rest of the sea. Rumors concerning our being stalked by German U-boats were substantiated when I observed the explosions of depth charges that were fired by the naval vessels accompanying us.

Although "I" Company worked in the galley, the British crew selected the menu, with one of the more unpleasant items on the menu being boiled bacon. This fatty item undoubtedly contributed to the seasickness besetting many of the troops.

The upper decks, which housed the officers, were strictly off-limits to enlisted personnel, and the imaginations of all of us who were of lower rank ran wild about the shenanigans that were likely taking place among those of the privileged classes. To keep us enlisted men occupied, there was little provided except supervised boxing matches, and gambling was always evident.

I proposed having a chess tournament, and the officer in charge thought this to be a worthwhile suggestion. Rather than merely announce over the public address system that a chess tournament would be held, he embellished his remarks by mentioning my name as challenging anyone on the ship to beat me! There was a sizable group of players eager to play against me. I was a competent amateur, but in no way did I intend, nor would I be able, to take on all comers in competition. After I explained to those assembled that the announcement was in error, everyone was willing to play just for fun without the pressure of a tournament setting.

Many long hours of leisure gave me the opportunity to do something I had always wanted to do, but never took the opportunity to achieve; namely, to read the New Testament in its entirety. I remember, back then, reading passages in its twenty-seven books that were unclear; but subsequent persistent study made the Scripture's infallibility self-evident. This experience was influential in my later embracing non-sectarian, Bible-believing Christianity, rather than denominational religion.

After an otherwise uneventful crossing, we arrived in Liverpool. Shortly after disembarking and leaving the dock, our ship sank in the harbor. We learned later that she was leaking, and the pumps were operating during the voyage to keep us afloat. Because of the danger of German submarine attack, leaving the safety of the convoy to return to port was not an option.

Chapter 20
Wales

We boarded double-decker buses and, traveling several hours through towns and villages that were ravaged by German air raids, arrived in Wales. I had never known of anyone else who was stationed in that country. We first were billeted in a castle, and the prospect of living in such an ancient edifice was appealing; but before the day ended, we left because it was rat-infested. We went next to a barrack that had been used by British troops, but was now abandoned. Its large room, which contained perhaps twenty cots, had a tiny stove at one end. There was a pile of pressed soft coal bricks in a bucket alongside of it, and the stove was large enough for only one brick, each one about the size of a bar of laundry soap. It was cold and rainy, as it was nearly every day during the month that we were in Wales, and the pitiable fire that could be maintained in the dinky stove was completely ineffectual. We were there no more than a day or so, until our three battalions were then transported to three towns on the outskirts of Swansea.

Our third battalion was stationed in Penclawdd, a charming little village of coal miners and diggers of mussels. For the entire time since I left the United States until arriving in Penclawdd, I did not once see Chaplain Morgan. Chaplain's assistants (CA's) were required to be armed with the M1 Garand rifle. The other chaplains went on the battle lines with one company or the other, and their assistants assumed the duty of another rifleman, with the ostensible role of protecting the chaplain.

Here was the dilemma: Chaplain Morgan always made his headquarters with the battalion aid station. He said that when we became engaged in battle, he wanted to be with the wounded to "comfort" them. Chaplains were not armed, but wore brassards emblazoned with a Red Cross on a white field, the identical symbol worn by medical personnel and on flags identifying aid stations. The Geneva Convention forbade any kind of weapon in an installation showing a Red Cross, the penalty for which was execution by firing squad. Morgan was obsessed by the fear of being taken prisoner by the Germans if he were protected by the Red Cross, and while being in my presence when I was carrying a firearm.

Morgan's solution to the problem was to have me assigned to a unit where he was not apt to be, and send a runner when he needed me to assist with a church service, drive him somewhere, type letters, or take care of whatever else he might want.

The unit chosen for me to stay, unless needed, was the battalion I&R (Intelligence and Reconnaissance) platoon. This was a wonderful group of men, and they welcomed me heartily, even though I had no official role in their unit. I was unfamiliar with how they patrolled enemy positions, or other aspects of gathering intelligence, and I felt like the proverbial "fifth wheel on a wagon." All of the men had some college background, and came from urban areas such as New York, Chicago, Boston, and Philadelphia. In each of the prior outfits to which I belonged, it took me a little while to establish close friendships among its soldiers, but after a few days I would always find one person with common interests, and such association helped to overcome the homesickness. With all the men of I&R, however, I felt an instant kinship that proved especially valuable during the uncertain times that would lie ahead.

We had no idea when, exactly, we would be leaving for the continent. The D-Day invasion had occurred five months earlier, and we anticipated joining the fray somewhere in France. In Penclawdd, our quarters, lavatory, and mess hall, occupied corrugated metal buildings. Another small village named Llanelly lay nearby, and the nearest town that could offer at least a modicum of excitement was Swansea.

The men of our platoon had little to do during the day, but the soldiers in the line companies maintained their physical condition by daily marches, and made final zeroing-in adjustments to their weapons' sights. I went to the motor pool to pick up a new jeep for the chaplain. He insisted that I get a Ford rather than a Willys. When the jeep was turned over to me, I was told to perform certain prescribed maintenance services. This meant checking fluid levels in the radiator, crankcase, transfer case, transmission, etc., and tightening all nuts, screws, and bolts on the engine, body, and chassis, checking tire pressure, and lubricating fittings throughout with the grease gun. These chores were to be done every day by every driver to whom a vehicle was entrusted. I knew, of course, that it was essential for basic concerns to be addressed, but I thought I could get away without spending the excessive effort to take care of all the nitpicky details.

The motor pool sergeant saw me preparing to leave the motor pool with my new jeep, and questioned my leaving so soon. He said that he didn't believe I could have performed all of the required maintenance in such a short time, but I assured him that I had done so. He asked to see the grease gun with which I was to have lubricated the fittings underneath the vehicle. Upon opening it, he saw that it still contained cosmoline, the heavy, gummy substance which was applied to metal when it was stored for any length of time to prevent rust and corrosion. There was no lubricating grease in the gun, and my duplicity was divulged. I was assailed with a diatribe of matchless profanities, and ordered to complete every element of required maintenance. From that time on, the sergeant harangued me constantly about every real or imagined vehicular problem, and demanded my attending to it immediately. I deserved being chastised, but his distrust and ill feeling never abated until months later, when he wanted me to act as interpreter to arrange dates between him and German girls. I didn't accede to his request, however, because a non-fraternization policy was declared, and any contact or association with German civilians was prohibited.

There was little to do in the nearby villages except drink beer or buy chips in a pub. I had heard about fish and chips before, but did not realize that chips were French fried potato sticks. These were dispensed in cones fashioned from newspaper pages. The fact that there was ink on the paper didn't bother us.

Swansea was a larger town somewhat farther away, and our trucks would provide us with transportation. We went to the movies, or we visited service clubs that were counterparts to our USO's in the States. The women were eager to be our dates, because there were not many able-bodied civilian men left in the country. It is not an exaggeration to say that well over half of all the girls—or women, if you prefer—had long, beautiful, bright red hair. The few Welshmen that remained resented deeply our encroachment on their territory, and a few altercations resulted. One of my friends and I were walking with a couple of women one evening, and were accosted by several young civilian Welshmen—three or four, I don't remember exactly how many—who threatened us, telling us to leave town. One of them had a knife. As they came within range, I grabbed one of them, throwing him to the ground. Someone on the street said, "Leave the Yanks alone," and the would-be assailants fled. In hindsight, it was foolhardy for me to react as I did; but in the words of the Bard, "All's Well That End's Well."

The different regiments and battalions were scattered among a number of towns in the area. Chaplain Morgan wanted me to take him to the picturesque town of Tenby located on the Bristol Channel. Whether it was our division or regimental headquarters, I no longer remember. Having just recently received my jeep, I had had few occasions until then to drive anywhere. No sooner did I proceed down the road, than a civilian automobile was approaching me head-on. The driver honked his horn and I honked mine, and we both swerved to avoid colliding. In an instant I realized that I was driving on the wrong side of the road. I soon became accustomed to driving on the left, but absentmindedly committed the same error on one or two other occasions. Fortunately, no harm resulted, but I noticed some irate gestures from the civilian natives. Cloverleaf intersections were a menace, too, but after a while, I learned to accommodate to them.

During the weeks in October, November, and part of December that we were in Wales, I saw the sun once. The weather was usually drizzling or foggy, and miserably chilly. Blackout conditions prevailed, and with the absence of visible lights in house windows, or streetlights, or cars with headlights, along with poor weather visibility, it was impossible to see anyone when walking at night. The civilians carried flashlights with discreetly dim illumination, powered by self-contained generators, activated by squeezing a hand lever. One could hear the quiet whir of the little generators, as pedestrians would approach.

Movies sometimes portray Welshmen, particularly coal miners, who sing in harmony as they march to work. This is not Hollywood fantasy; the Welsh are really a nation of singers. I attended Sunday services at a church in Penclawdd in which the congregation sat in sections according to whether they were sopranos, altos, tenors, or basses, and the hymn singing was magnificent.

I was unable to read the music notation in the hymnal; it was unlike anything I had seen up to that time. Rather than consisting of notes represented by dots on a lined staff with which most people are familiar, the notation comprised letters of the alphabet, colons, commas, and dashes. It is a system called "tonic-sol-fa," and has been used for generations throughout the British Empire. Its most prevalent occurrence is in choral music, rather than instrumental. Briefly, the letters are abbreviations for the Italian syllables, "do-re-mi," etc. which are taught to children even here in America. The British use these letters, along with punctuation signs denoting rhythmic elements, to create a marvelously simple and elegant method of showing choristers what to sing.

The syllables may also be translated into hand gestures whereby a choir director merely thrusts his hand and fingers in a prescribed position that designates the note to be sung. By using two hands, one who is adept in this skill can direct two divisions of a group, each singing a different part, simultaneously. The beauty and simplicity of the system, whether written or manual, is that singers recognize, instantly and accurately, precisely what tonal pitches are intended. I was so impressed with "tonic-sol-fa," that I wrote a manual in graduate school, advocating its adoption in the United States. Nothing came of my effort, however, because our traditional notation was too thoroughly entrenched.

On one of the Sundays that I attended the church, a choir rehearsal was scheduled after the service to prepare for the Christmas presentation of *Messiah*, the oratorio by George Frederick Handel. No one left the church; everyone was a choir member!

When he heard about my music background and career plans, the organist invited me to play for one of the services. I invited a couple of my soldier friends to go with me to church, and we were invited by the organist to visit his home one evening for supper. With the difficult times brought about by the war, rationing was severe. This Welsh family's need to use their resources sparingly was demonstrated when our host buttered the bread before cutting a sheer sliver, in order to avoid tearing it, which could happen if such a thin piece were buttered after slicing.

We had a nice chat after eating, and spent the evening playing the piano for each other. As we prepared to leave, our host handed me one of his calling cards. It contained his name, Gwynfor Jenkins—"Jenkins" being as common a name in Wales as Smith or Jones are in America—and the name of the organization to which he belonged: "Independent Order of Rechabites." He announced proudly that its members must never in their lives have imbibed any alcoholic beverage. Not until later, when I became more familiar with the Scriptures, did I recognize that in Jeremiah 35:5–7 the Rechabites were a Jewish sect who abstained from drinking wine, and refused to live in houses; they resided in tents. If I knew this when I talked with Mr. Jenkins, I would have asked him how he rationalized having a house, thereby straying from this vital requirement of Rechab's followers.

Chapter 21

To the Continent

Word finally arrived that we were to leave Penclawdd. We were allowed passes to the village, but for reasons of security, were ordered not to tell the village folks that we were to ship out. When we arrived, everybody already knew that we were to leave the area. How did they know? Somebody, somewhere, passed the word to them.

We bade our farewells and returned for our last night in camp before leaving the British Isles. The next day everyone was packed and ready to leave, when it was announced that we would remain another day. Again, passes were issued, and when we went to the village, all of its residents were happy again to see us, and said that they knew we would be back. Some military secrecy!

Our convoy of military vehicles headed for Southampton, England. I do not know how many regiments of the division were in the convoy, but it was impressive, with jeeps and their trailers, two-and-a-half ton trucks, three-quarter ton trucks, ambulances, and weapons carriers. Again, my chaplain was not with me, but traveled with other officers in the battalion, such as the commander (a major), his adjutant with the rank of captain, and first lieutenant Kennedy, the intelligence officer, known as S2.

Every vehicle in the convoy was required to have a driver and assistant driver. Since the chaplain did not accompany me, someone was to be chosen to occupy the right seat of my jeep. Selected to be my assistant was Dino Argentini, with whom I still communicate at the time of this writing. He was a member of I&R, and was designated as the battalion sniper. He carried an M1 as his regular weapon, but for greater accuracy needed for sniping, he had access to a 1903 Springfield bolt-action rifle. Later on he acquired a Thompson sub-machinegun from a soldier who was sent back for medical treatment after being wounded. I also came into possession of a Thompson, but when the battalion commander saw it, he took it from me because the army TO (table of organization) specified that I be armed with an M1 rifle. I was hoping to take it home after the war. What a souvenir that would have been!

We left Wales and traveled for two days across southern England, staying one night at a British army barrack. Arriving at port, we boarded an LST, the naval vessel with the drop-front ramp that was used for landing assault troops on beaches. After we drove our vehicles into the hold, they were fastened with chains to prevent them from moving out of place if the sea were rough.

The English Channel was calm and the crossing uneventful. There was the possibility, even this long after the initial invasion, that ships crossing the channel could be attacked by German warplanes. The LST was under the command of the U.S. navy, and we asked one of the sailors about the 20-millimeter anti-aircraft guns located on deck. He volunteered to demonstrate how the cartridges were loaded into the gun in readiness to be fired. He took a magazine from a rack and attempted to insert it into the gun. It became jammed, and wouldn't go in, nor would it come out. He attempted to cock the weapon, but the mechanism did not budge. Upon examination, the weapon's moving parts were found to be still encased in protective cosmoline, the substance mentioned earlier, found in the grease gun when I was supposed to have lubricated my jeep. Had our LST been attacked, its anti-aircraft gun would have been useless.

We disembarked on French soil later than expected because we entered via the Seine River, arriving at the city of Rouen, rather than on the coast. Our convoy continued across France until reaching Fréville, a farming hamlet where we assembled, waiting for orders to enter enemy territory.

It had rained heavily, and we were camped in a sea of mud. The wooden shoes worn by the French peasants were practical when walking through the mire. I did not realize before, that Netherlanders were not the only people who wore wooden clogs. The ground was so soggy that tent pins would not hold our shelter halves in place. There was no place to sleep except to place one's raincoat on the sloppy mess and lie on it. We remained in the area for several days, and I slept in my jeep. It was a miserable, sleepless experience because there was no place to stretch out. I tried lying across the rear seat, but it was too short, and required moving a duffle bag, ammunition box, gas mask, and other assorted paraphernalia to some other location. I had heard that some of the men rented barn haylofts from the civilians, and followed their example. The farmers were afraid of fire, and warned us against smoking in the barns.

Although still reasonably far away from front lines, a number of soldiers were visibly worried when thinking about the inevitable contact with enemy forces. One soldier in our camp shot himself in the foot, hoping to be sent home. He said that it was an accident resulting from cleaning his rifle, but no one was convinced that his claim was true. He was treated by the medics and returned to duty. I heard a couple of fellows also toying with the idea of wounding themselves, hoping to be exempted from combat, and the viewpoint that prevailed was that it would require the so-called "million dollar wound" to be sent home. Such a wound was one that broke the femur, or thighbone. It would heal after a while and one could walk again, but the recovery time would not make return to combat duty feasible.

Even though the notion of being in action was not something to be anticipated, I was eager to leave this sea of muck. My twentieth birthday occurred here, but I wasn't thinking about dates, and forgot all about it!

It was time to move on, and our convoy continued closer to the front. Battles were raging some distance from us, and we could hear artillery in the distance, and at night, we saw tracer bullets from friend and foe alike in the sky. As Dino and I drove through towns and villages where hardly anything was left standing, we did not know whether we were still in France, or whether we had reached Holland or Belgium. Dino knew a little French, and as we passed people along the road, he yelled to them, asking our location. Since we did not understand them, we assumed we were no longer in France.

Each day, as we came nearer German lines, there was the wonderful sight of thousands of our B-17 bombers in formation on their way to destroy German industrial sites. German fighter planes attacked them, and American fighter escorts challenged them in dogfights. It was a frightful experience to watch our bombers systematically destroyed. Some exploded in flight, while others tumbled from the sky, with their crews sometimes parachuting to safety.

On one such foray I was aghast to see many more planes than usual dropping out of formation. I looked intently on one particular silvery crippled aircraft as it plummeted towards earth, and it was going to strike where I was standing! I was mesmerized by the approaching mass until it came within a few inches of my face! How could this be? What I saw was a fragment of metallic chaff that was released from our bombers to confuse enemy radar. My distance perception was skewed because, when I first saw the glistening metal, it was a few hundred feet above me. Being light in weight, it floated slowly, creating the optical illusion of being an aircraft. Happily, this was just a delusion, but I saw many other real airplanes engulfed in smoke and flames, tumbling out of control and impacting the earth.

When our convoy stopped at night, a guard detail protected the men and equipment from either civilian or enemy incursions into our midst. All of us took turns as sentinels, on duty for two hours, and off for four hours, and we repeated this schedule through the night.

It was my turn to stand guard, and we were warned that German paratroopers were dropped into our area, and to be on the lookout for them. I was replacing as a sentinel my good friend, Ward Brunner, my classmate at CCNY, and who was now a machine gunner in "M" Company's heavy weapons platoon. I asked him what he would do if he were on sentry duty, and saw a German paratrooper standing right in front of him. Without hesitation he replied,"I'd shoot the son-of-a-bitch!" That seemed reasonable to me, although I was concerned, for fear the paratrooper were not alone. If other Germans were nearby, then what would I do? Fortunately, I did not have to contend with that situation just yet. This was a grace period that my inexperience welcomed, but the time was to come when confrontation with the enemy was not hypothetical.

Chapter 22

Contact at Last

The chaplain finally rejoined me as we kept heading east towards the front lines. I wondered how we would know what to do when we encountered the enemy. Would someone in authority order us to take positions and attack? Would we wait to be attacked? The answer I received was never definitive: we keep going until we meet him.

I had not heard that there was a breakthrough by a massive German onslaught headed in our direction, but our division leaders most certainly were aware of the "Belgian Bulge," the last desperate intrusion ordered by Hitler to annihilate the Allied Forces once and for all.

It was December 23rd, and the ever-present sounds of distant explosions indicated that we would see action very soon. A church service was announced with Captain Morgan, the battalion Protestant chaplain, presiding. A Catholic Mass with Chaplain Lang was also scheduled.

As was my custom when a worship service was scheduled, I hauled from the trailer towed behind my jeep, the carton of hymnals and the little field organ. The instrument was a diminutive form of the reed parlor organs that were used in homes a generation earlier. Wind was provided with pedals, and despite its small size, the sound was quite beautiful and remarkably loud.

The service was held in a barn, and jammed to capacity. I was told later that no one was absent from the services, either Protestant or Catholic. The spirits of the men were high, and the singing was enthusiastic. Later on, services were conducted among individual companies when there was a lull in battle; and never were there more than perhaps two or three soldiers in an entire company who stayed away.

The following day, Christmas Eve, we continued heading towards the German lines, and many of the vehicles were adorned with sprigs of greenery taken from the forest through which we were traveling. Men were singing Christmas carols, and appeared astonishingly happy and confident as they approached an uncertain future.

Snow was beginning to fall. Our convoy was on a narrow road near the town of Grandmenil, Belgium. Darkness fell, but silhouetted vehicles were visible against the snow. When our convoy came to a halt, the chaplain left the jeep and told me to remain with it. He said he was going to battalion headquarters, which was in a house that sat alone in the woods, to find out what was happening. He told me to get his bedroll from the jeep, and he took it with him, expecting to sleep inside out of the cold. Officers' bedrolls were thick and wonderfully warm, compared to the enlisted men's pathetically thin, unlined sleeping bags.

Every jeep and truck had a driver and an

assistant driver, but I was the only person alone in a vehicle. As the convoy sat parked along the edge of the road, Sherman tanks came from behind and passed us, heading up the hill towards the town. The road was narrow, and a tank collided with my trailer, tearing its tarpaulin cover. I was in no position to do anything about the damage, nor could anything I said be heard, because of the din of roaring engines and clanking tank treads. The convoy remained parked on the road, and I tried to sleep, sitting in the driver's seat.

Artillery, mortar, rifle, and machine gun fire could be heard not very far away, and sleep was fitful. It was evident that something significant was going on a bit farther up the road. The noise of weapons was becoming louder and more frequent. From out of nowhere, German King Tiger tanks were on the road in front of me. I did not see them earlier because it was dark, and there was a bend in the road, which kept them from view. Two of my friends were in the fourth or fifth jeep in front of mine. As a tank came alongside of them, a German soldier in the open hatch of the turret, dropped a "potato masher" grenade into the jeep, and it landed on the driver's seat. The grenade blew up, killing my friend instantly. I did not see this as it was happening, but I saw the assistant driver a few minutes later. He was wounded slightly, and told me details about the incident.

I saw the first tank as it faced the jeep two vehicles ahead of my own, perhaps two hundred feet or so. The tank drove right over that jeep and rotated in one direction and then the other, squashing it until the whole vehicle—including its engine—was crushed to within a few inches of the ground. The tank continued in my direction and crushed the jeep immediately in front of mine. I ran from my jeep and jumped into a ditch by the side of the road, realizing that I was next in line for destruction.

In the terror of the first contact with the enemy, one of the men who was alongside the tank fired his bazooka at it; but he forgot to pull the safety pin, and the bazooka's missile bounced harmlessly off the side. This error was immediately noticed, and a second bazooka round was fired and exploded as intended. Sadly, however, the one who fired was too close to the tank, and the blast from the exploding missile killed him. Someone else fired another bazooka round, and it struck the tank in the rear, stopping its engine. The other tanks fled back from where they came. I climbed back out of the ditch and was relieved to see that my jeep was still intact.

It remained a mystery what became of the occupants in the damaged tank. I heard—and believed it until recently—that they escaped from a hatch in the bottom of the tank, and ran into the woods. One of my present friends, a German tank commander in the war, told me that there was no outlet in the bottom of the tank.

When the Germans retreated, our infantrymen continued their pursuit into the town—more properly, a village—of Grandmenil. No purpose would have been served by the convoy's following immediately into the village where street fighting was taking place, so we were to remain with the vehicles, awaiting further instructions.

Seeing no reason to sit there doing nothing, I walked a few hundred yards to a house that displayed the Red Cross banner denoting our battalion aid station, and found surgeon Captain T.D. Allison, medical administrative officer Lieutenant Greiner, Chaplain Morgan, and several medical corps enlisted men, who were tending the wounded. I was surprised that no one made an issue of my being in the aid station with my rifle, considering the Geneva Convention edict that forbade weapons in a medical facility.

I made myself useful, holding blood plasma bottles high and upright so that the fluid could flow into the patients' veins. After seeing dead Americans and Germans from the earlier firefight, and being among more dead and wounded in the aid station, I became queasy. After initial exposure to blood and torn flesh, however, my discomfort abated quickly. I reflected on these unfortunates, as compared to my having been spared death or injury, and I was eager to assist where possible.

Sometime later, after seeing numerous battle casualties, I was examining the dog tags around the neck of a slain soldier in order to identify him. While reaching my hand under his jacket, shirt, and undershirt with one hand, I was eating something, holding it with the other hand. A fellow who observed me expressed amazement that I didn't lose my appetite.

I admired Captain Allison's poised demeanor

as he skillfully removed shrapnel fragments from the numerous patients who were carried in on litters by the medics. These heroes worked tirelessly on the battlefield, armed with nothing more than their Red Cross armbands. One soldier was brought in who was shot in the stomach. The bullet did not penetrate very far because it was made of wood, and light in weight. It was blue in color and of small caliber, and it broke in half with splintered edges at the fracture. The surgeon described it as a dum-dum, the use of which is forbidden by the Geneva Convention. Technically, however, it was not a true dum-dum, because it did not have a steel base and an expanding soft metal core.

The wounded were often administered morphine for pain by medics on the battlefield. After arriving at the aid station they were treated by the doctor, and if their wounds were severe enough to warrant being sent back to a field hospital, they were usually given a blue capsule to sedate them en route. They were always warned to remain seated while waiting for the ambulance, because this medicine put them almost immediately in a stupor. I saw a few soldiers staggering helplessly until they collapsed as the medicine took effect.

When daylight arrived, the adjutant, Captain Willoughby Tyler, wanted to go to up the road to see the aftermath of the previous night's battle. Other officers from the battalion and the regiment also went to examine the scene. There was a shortage of jeeps caused by the German tanks' assault, but since mine was unscathed, I was chosen to drive the captain up the mountain. The devastation was horrific. Something—mortar or artillery fire—hit our ammunition truck, and the fire that resulted caused whatever ammunition that remained in the truck to explode, with missiles and shrapnel being hurled at random intervals in all directions. No one dared go near it. Dead men lay everywhere, and many of those who survived removed their backpacks, abandoning them because they were an encumbrance.

The Germans were gone from the area, but we were told that we must always expect a counterattack; and the enemy was certain to be not too far ahead of us. As we looked at the destruction and carnage, I felt a sense of security because a half dozen or so of our P-38 Lightning fighter planes were flying around above us, apparently patrolling the skies looking for targets of opportunity. These aircraft were not as prevalent as were the P-51 Mustang or the P-47 Thunderbolt; but they were my favorite airplane of the war. Their twin fuselage and twin engines gave them a sleek, classy appearance; and their great speed, .50-caliber machine guns, and bomb load made them a formidable foe. The Germans referred to them as twin-tailed devils, and expressed incredulity that one pilot was capable of handling all of this airplane and its armament.

The flaming ammunition truck and a couple of others atop the mountain had fluorescent panels draped over their cab roofs. These bright, colorful sheets showed our airplanes that the vehicles were American. They also served as a demarcation between our lines and the enemy's. Without giving this function of the panels any thought, we left our jeeps and were walking around on the enemy's side of the panels. Suddenly I heard machine gun fire and the roar of engines. The planes overhead, assuming we were Germans, strafed us, and dropped bombs on the road. For a moment, it did not occur to me that the gunfire was coming from our own planes; I thought the Germans were counterattacking in force. When everyone realized that it was friendly fire, all of us dove for cover, such as it was, alongside the road.

One after the other, each plane dove at us, then climbed up and returned for another strafing run. As I lay at the side of the road, I looked up and saw one of the planes dropping its bomb on our position. Instinctively I put my head down and, peeking from under the brim of my steel helmet, saw holes being made in the road as the .50-caliber bullets were fired at us.

A major—I never found out who he was— stood in the road, waving his map board in a futile effort to signal the diving aircraft that we were not the enemy. A bomb was released from one of the planes and, landing close to him, blew him to smithereens! Truly, he was a self-sacrificing hero. I thought that the attack would never end, and felt that I would not survive it.

Someone with access to a radio called head-quarters, but the line of communication went from battalion to regiment, to division, to corps, and finally to the air force. Only then were the planes overhead directed to call off their attack. It is no wonder that the assault seemed interminable.

As I lay there, another soldier was alongside me. I was between him and the road where the bullets and bombs were impacting. He let out a yell, saying that he was hit. His trousers were torn and blood was seeping from a thigh wound, apparently caused by shrapnel from one of the bombs. How he was struck, with my being closer to the exploding bomb than he was, I was never able to understand.

Immediately I called for a medic. The medic looked over at us briefly to ascertain the seriousness of the wound, and said that it was more urgent to tend to another casualty. I went over to the man with the more serious wound, and saw that his entire arm, from elbow to his neck, was missing its flesh. Nothing but bones and ligaments were showing, and steam was coming off what was left of the arm because it was cold. It was Christmas Day.

The wounded needed to be taken back down the mountain for medical care, and everyone else was eager to leave the area. I ran back to where I left the jeep, and was relieved to discover that it was untouched by the planes. Captain Tyler got alongside me in the jeep, and no fewer than eight other soldiers joined us. There was normally room for a driver and three passengers, but some sat on the hood so that I could hardly see where I was driving. Some sat on top of each other on the back seat, and others sat on the spare tire in the back, while others sat on the storage bins on each side of the rear seat.

I was in a hurry to get out of the area, not wanting to fall victim to an enemy attack with too few soldiers among the few of us to put up an effective fight. There was snow on the ground, and the road was slippery. I sped down the precipitous road, skidding precariously, and scaring the men almost as much as the attack a few moments ago. Captain Tyler patted me reassuringly on the arm, and said something on the order of, "O.K., Birkby, just take it easy, take it easy. We want to get there in one piece."

Chapter 23
Smell of Death

I was in an infantry division, and earned the Combat Infantryman's Badge (It paid an additional ten dollars a month). I shot at the enemy, and the enemy shot at me; but as a chaplain's assistant, I was not expected to make first contact with the Germans in any of our encounters. My admiration of riflemen was enhanced whenever I was subjected to any of the plights that they endured, and I experienced them on numerous occasions.

The administrative officer, Lieutenant Greiner, would go to the next town or village that our troops occupied, and from which the Germans were expelled, to seek a house that was suitable for setting up an aid station. As previously noted, the chaplain was invariably with the battalion aid station. There was hardly a time, therefore, when he was not in an enclosure that was often heated.

I was made to stand outside in blizzard conditions because, as already noted, the chaplain wanted to avoid breaking the Geneva Convention rules by having armed personnel (me) under the protection of a medical facility. I tried to sneak in for a few moments of relief from the cold, but the chaplain, using his favorite expletive, would yell, "Dadgummit, Art, I told you to stay out of here!"

I appreciated the plight of the line company soldier who was never warm. When the chaplain did not need me for anything, I got relief from the frigid conditions by staying with the I&R platoon, usually headquartered in a billet, a house the Germans might have occupied before being ousted by our troops.

When it was certain that the Germans were driven out of Grandmenil, the hamlet just beyond where the bombing and strafing occurred, the I&R platoon moved into a farmhouse located there. One of the first things that required attention was removal of the corpses. There are few smells more repugnant to me than the strangely sweetish odor of decaying dead bodies. We laid our fallen soldiers in rows inside a barn, and the graves registration personnel from division headquarters came by later to take the bodies for burial. German soldiers were literally thrown into piles like firewood, and I never learned what measures were taken for their removal.

There was a dead German lying at the bottom of a huge bomb crater that I would estimate to be fifteen feet deep and thirty feet in diameter. I was reluctant to remove the body, lest it be booby-trapped. Setting explosives under corpses was a common practice by the Germans. I told a couple of German prisoners to go down into the crater to extricate the body; and I told them why I was not going to do it. They, too, were fearful, but knew that they had to comply. They tied a rope to the corpse to retrieve it, but there was no booby trap. I was informed later that the rules of war prohibited subjecting prisoners to this kind of potential danger. I also was unaware that it was unlawful for us to get low to the ground when artillery was coming in, and to make enemy prisoners remain standing unprotected, but this was common practice.

There was always concern that snipers might be in the area, so we went with an armed companion to keep watch whenever we squatted down over a slit trench to relieve ourselves. On one occasion our battalion commander asked me to accompany him as a guard while he dug a trench and defecated in the woods. Amazing! Even senior officers have to go, just like enlisted men!

Orders were given that if there were a counterattack, we were to hold our position in the village, whatever the cost. I went upstairs and looked out a window, planning my response to a possible return of the Germans. I looked for a good spot to pick them off, hoping they would be standing up in their tank turret. Other options came to mind: What if the hatches were closed? What if a large number of tanks came? Was I more vulnerable upstairs or in the cellar if a tank fired its cannon or machinegun? This was one of several similar quandaries I experienced where I was not an integral part of an armed unit, such as a rifle squad, whose actions were directed or coordinated by a knowledgeable tactician. The chaplain certainly could not fill that role, and I&R was not intended for a direct close-combat confrontation with enemy troops.

There was a beautiful church in this little hamlet. Bullets severely damaged it, and artillery made a hole at least ten feet in diameter in one of the walls. My friend, Dino, the battalion sniper who was my assistant driver when we left Wales, loved music, and knew that I could play the organ. He suggested that we go to the church and try out its instrument. It was immediately apparent that many pipes were damaged. We were warned that the Germans often set booby traps whenever they vacated a location, and we were shown during our stateside training how to be on the lookout for them. Accordingly, Dino and I ascended the spiral staircase leading to the organ loft, and searched the organ thoroughly to ascertain whether explosives may have been placed under the keyboards, under the organ bench, or inside the casework enclosing the bulk of the organ.

Finding nothing suspicious, I sat at the console, and Dino went behind the organ to pump the bellows with a hand crank, there being no electric motor to provide wind. Not completely confident that no danger lurked by way of booby-traps, I gingerly pressed the topmost key of the console. At that very instant there was a tremendous explosion, and we believed that the Germans had, indeed, returned with a vengeance. We grabbed our rifles, raced down the stairs, and exited the church. Rather than the enemy's return, we saw that a cow had stepped on one of our anti-tank mines and was blown to kingdom come.

We remained for several days in Grandmenil, and had little to do except wait for further orders. Livestock were roaming loose, and to prevent animals from setting off our mines, as had happened outside the church, we herded them into a cemetery enclosed by a low stone fence. With the cattle confined, we decided to have some fresh milk. No one in our group had any farm experience. I had watched cows being milked when I visited a farm as a kid, and volunteered to do the job. I isolated a cow from the rest of the animals, and, using my helmet to catch the milk, manipulated the udder in what I perceived to be a logical means of extracting the liquid. It was more difficult than I imagined it to be, and could only get less than a quart.

I was concerned that the milk might be contaminated, because the farming that was carried on in this area was not likely to have the high standards of dairy production found back home. To safeguard our health, we heated the milk as a form of primitive pasteurization and added sugar from our rations to improve its taste. I did not realize that milk commercially produced back home was strained, and the milk that we obtained from our cow had hair in it. The heated milk and sugar concoction tasted awful, and I felt sick after drinking some of it.

We treated ourselves to fruit preserves and homemade bread that were in the cellar of our billet. It was tasty, but the bread contained stone particles that came from the millstone used to grind the grain. We thought it would provide beneficial dietary roughage, and ate it with no ill effect.

While we were biding our time in the hamlet, awaiting orders to move on, a United States Air

Force officer walked into our headquarters. He was attired in "pinks," the regulation dress uniform for officers. We were nowhere near an air force establishment, and were astonished to see air force personnel under this circumstance. He claimed that he was shot down somewhere—and he mentioned the specific location—many miles away, and walked until he found us. We immediately were suspicious of his story because his uniform was clean, and he gave no impression of having, indeed, traveled far on foot. Believing him to be a German spy, we questioned him at length about his role in the military, and about civilian topics with which any American should be familiar. We asked him about American movies, sports personalities and events, historical topics, and anything else that might reveal his being an interloper. He never faltered in any answer, so we were left with little alternative but to release him to battalion headquarters, and let them handle the situation appropriately. Nothing further about this incident was ever brought to our attention.

This was the first place where we encountered German V-1 buzz bombs. One would hear the growling, low-pitched rumble of the engine as the flying, unmanned missile approached. Everyone rushed into the house to avoid being harmed by this innovative weapon. Suddenly, the engine stopped, and the bomb fell instantly to the earth, exploding with great devastation. Buzz bombs could not be sent to any location with accuracy, and their point of impact was random. I heard a number of them and saw one in flight, but I never heard about any of our troops being harmed by them. It was reported that our division anti-aircraft guns were the first ever to shoot a buzz bomb from the sky.

The Ardennes campaign, known popularly as the "Battle of the Bulge," is recognized as being one of the greatest battles in all of history. The 75th Division was thrown into this fray to turn back the last desperation thrust by Hitler to break through our lines and win the eventual victory. For our role in defeating the Germans, we were nicknamed the "Bulge Busters." Our division contained the youngest average age personnel of all military outfits, and we were also known as the "Diaper Division."

While battalion intelligence officer, First Lieutenant Kennedy, was on a scouting mission, his jeep ran over a German mine and was damaged beyond repair. The lieutenant suffered a shoulder injury and his driver, Francis Bond, was severely wounded. I watched as Bond was put into the ambulance for transfer to the hospital. He moaned over and over, "Oh, my back, my back!" Shortly thereafter we received word that he died en route. Not too long before, a group of us were talking about religion. There were the usual opinions offered concerning either the validity or foolishness of belief in God, and Bond said, "I don't believe in nothin'!" How tragic!

Word came to battalion headquarters that one of the line companies was pinned down by enemy fire. It was unable to move, and the men ran out of food. Lieutenant Kennedy's arm was in a sling following his jeep's being blown up, but he remained on duty. He was assigned the task of taking rations to the pinned down company, but he had no jeep and his driver was dead. He asked Chaplain Morgan whether I could drive him (Kennedy) with the rations to the stricken company, and the chaplain readily agreed.

Kennedy piled several cases of rations in my jeep, and we headed for the woods. The lieutenant was only nineteen years old, but he must have been wise beyond his years to become the battalion intelligence officer. He directed me through the forest where there were no actual roads, but rather faint paths that other vehicles had made through the trees.

The snow was deep and the night was dark. I had no idea where I was or where I was headed. Kennedy would tell me, for example, that there was a large fallen tree up ahead, or that there was a lone shack ahead of us on the right. Sure enough, he knew every detail of the area.

After several miles of my following his directions, Kennedy told me to be aware of an American tank on the left, a little distance ahead. There, as promised, sat a Sherman tank with a crewman in the turret. I stopped, and the tanker demanded, "What's the password?"

I responded, "Dolphin." Then I asked him, "What's the countersign?"

He said, "What's the rest of the password?"

I answered, "I've identified who I am by giving you the password. It's your place to give me the countersign so that I know who you are."

Again the tanker demanded, "Give me all of it!" And again, I tried to explain to him that I had no way of knowing his identity, and that he had the obligation to give me the countersign. At this point, he turned the .50-caliber machine gun mounted on the turret directly at me, pulled the cocking lever, and told me to answer, or he would shoot. What to do? I was in his direct line of fire.

The lieutenant spoke up and said, "I'm an American officer, and I'm going to come over to you without a weapon, and talk." He walked around to the left side of the jeep where I was sitting, and with his hands up, approached the tank. Kennedy calmly explained the procedure about the need for both parties to give and take the elements of a password and its countersign. Due in part to the lieutenant's patience, and possibly due to his vulnerability being unarmed, the tanker finally comprehended the need for his response, and he acknowledged the counter-sign to be "Blue."

I find it interesting that I was often fearful, although armed with my rifle, when I was in defen-sive mode, so to speak. If I were ordered to act aggressively in the company of other soldiers, I felt an exhilaration and confidence, no matter what the danger. A dilemma where I was afraid because I had no backup, occurred when I was told to take a couple of medics in my jeep and pick up a few wounded sol-diers to be taken to the aid station. Not wanting the jeep to be seen and fired upon, I remained secluded in a hollow while the medics went out to the battlefield with litters. I was alone, and while waiting for them to return, I heard the firing of a German "burp gun" nearby. ("Burrrrp" was the distinctive sound of this small, handheld machine gun.) Were I with other armed soldiers, and if we encountered enemy troops, I could take appropriate action to kill them, and defend myself. Being alone, it was obvious I would have no chance of survival.

After what seemed to be an interminable wait, the medics returned with two wounded men. Their litters were laid across the jeep's hood, and I took them to the aid station without further incident.

In contrast with the above predicament was the time I was directed to accompany a squad to look for snipers. The enemy had been, for all intents and purposes, driven from a village, the name of which I no longer recall (there were so many of them). The chaplain said to me, "Art, get your gun. You're going hunting!" My rifle was in its usual place in the gun rack above the jeep's dashboard. I extracted it, and felt a genuine elation in this potentially deadly assign-ment, because I was with others who were armed.

We searched up and down the streets and house to house, going up and down stairs, from basements to attics. At one house, I heard Germans talking in a basement. I was one of three German interpreters for the battalion, so I yelled down the basement in Ger-man that I was going to throw a hand grenade down there, and if anyone were there, he was to come up. Instantly, several German soldiers came up the stairs with their hands behind their heads. One of them, an officer, was armed with a P-38 automatic pistol, the official German sidearm that replaced the famous Luger. I would have preferred having a Luger, but the P-38 was purportedly more accurate and reliable. Some time earlier I acquired a smaller-caliber, compact automatic that I was going to keep as a souvenir. I was told that anyone who was captured, and in possession of an enemy firearm, was subject to execution. Not wanting to face this possibility, I sold it to a willing buyer who was not worried about such circumstance. In the case of the P-38, I put aside my concern about being a prisoner, and kept the weapon hidden among my belongings in the jeep, and did not carry it on my person. This pistol, a swastika armband, and a heavy steel chain to which handgrips were attached to each end, were the only combat souvenirs that I brought home after the war. The Gestapo used the chain device as a "persuader" by wrapping it around a victim's wrist, and twisting it until confession was made or bones were broken.

Yet another occasion when I felt in high spirits was when I was with a group looking over an open area between two groves of trees. There were supposed to be no enemy in this immediate area, but from seemingly out of nowhere, several enemy soldiers exited from a stand of trees and ran across the field for cover on the other side. The moment we saw the fleeing soldiers, we fired offhand—that is, from a standing position without support for our rifles—dropping them in their tracks. When I am asked whether I ever shot anyone, I mention this incident in which my firing may, or may not have been responsible for my killing anyone.

In one town from which the Germans were not yet driven out, a runner came to me, telling me to report to the chaplain at the aid station. I ran from I&R to the aid station located a few blocks away, and a burst of German machine gun fire struck a low concrete wall alongside of me. I saw the wall being chipped away by the bullets, and I leaped over the wall to safety. I did not clear the top entirely, and cracked my shin on the corner of the wall as I fell to the other side. Someone put the machine gunner that was shooting at me out of action, and I continued on my way to see the chaplain. To this day I have a scar on my leg where the flesh was torn to the bone, my only wound in the war.

I learned later that such injury would merit the Purple Heart, but I did not ask about it at the time, believing that a wound had to be inflicted specifically by an enemy weapon rather than as a related injury. Another close call happened when shrapnel tore a hole in the sleeve of my combat jacket, but missed hitting my arm.

When I met with the chaplain, following my near miss with the machine gunner, he told me to get his map board from the jeep. There was no practical purpose for his having a map board; he played no role in military tactics or strategy. As I started out the door to go to the jeep, a round from an 88-millimeter artillery piece shrieked past and exploded nearby. I jumped back indoors, and the chaplain told me again to get the map board. More shells zipped past the door, and were destroying buildings and vehicles in the neighborhood. I told the chaplain I would wait until the firing stopped, whereupon he barked, "Get out there and do what I tell you. That's an order!"

Whatever the consequences from disobeying, I realized that his request was not vital to anyone's safety or the accomplishing of a mission, and I said that I would not go out under the present conditions. He stomped over to the door and said, "Well, I'll get it, then!" As he was about to go outside, another shell from the 88 streaked past and exploded. The chaplain said, "I suppose it can wait for the time being." The others in the room witnessed what happened, and their opinion of the chaplain, already less than admiring, became even lower.

The other chaplains in the battalion were highly esteemed by the troops. I saw Chaplain Prentis on more than one occasion marching with one company or another as they were heading for the front lines to engage the enemy. Chaplain Lang was conducting Mass for our troops in a bombed-out church, when mortar shells poured into town. Everybody in the church ducked down under the pews as glass and plaster were crashing to the floor, but Lang strode up and down the aisle, saying Mass without hesitation or revealing any hint of fear.

During this bombardment I was in a house struck by mortars. Debris and broken glass covered my helmet, but I was unscathed. German aircraft were also in the vicinity, dropping bombs. One of the bombs, weighing several hundred pounds, landed right outside the window of the room in which I was, but did not detonate; it was a dud.

Chaplain Lang won the Silver Star for bravery when he relayed wounded soldiers between a house and an ambulance, filling in for medics who, even though their Red Cross insignias were plainly visible on their helmets and their armbands, were killed by German snipers.

There were two kinds of engagements that gave me a real thrill, and earned "Hoorays" from all who witnessed them. One such event was seeing a wooded area in which the enemy was hiding, being bombarded by our artillery. Salvos of 105, and 155 millimeter, cannon fire would rake a selected expanse of forest, and puffs of smoke from the exploding shells, with hardly any space between them, would pound the landscape. How anyone could survive this concentrated pummeling is difficult to imagine!

The other event that elicited our cheers was watching our fighter planes, usually P-47's or P-38's, dive-bombing German tanks. Enemy tanks were not usually vulnerable to anything less than direct bomb or artillery hits. To witness an explosive flash and the virtual disappearance of an impenetrable piece of armored invincibility is an unforgettable sight!

On one occasion a half dozen or so of us were in a little stone farmhouse in a lightly wooded area, when we heard the sound of airplane engines. We rushed outside and saw a German and an American plane engaged in a dogfight. It was a spectacular sight as one and then the other would gain the advantage, diving at each other. At one point of the skirmish, the German pilot flew right towards us as we stood near the door of the farmhouse. The American pilot was right on his tail and fired his machine guns. The bullets tore up the ground in front of us, and we all ran to the door seeking cover. Three or four of us reached the open door at the same instant, and were jammed together so that no one could get through. It reminded me of the *Three Stooges*. All of us escaped being struck, and the planes flew out of sight, without our knowing the outcome of their dogfight.

Chapter 24
Going South

After having successfully turned back the German bulge, we went to another trouble spot known as the "Colmar Pocket" in the Alsace region of France. The area changed its allegiance between France and Germany for many generations. We were in ostensibly friendly territory belonging to France, but the civilian population included many Germans, and its dislike for Americans was palpable. It was still winter as we convoyed through the Vosges Mountains. The road was slippery and steep, and there were few guardrails.

I noticed a truck, several vehicles ahead of me, attempt to take a curve, but it went off the road and fell into an abyss down the mountain. The vehicle following was a jeep, pulling a trailer. In its attempt to negotiate the curve, it too went over the edge, falling into oblivion. There was little to be done about these casualties. We were going down a mountain, and there was no place to stop. It was my turn to enter the curve. Seeing what had happened to the unfortunates in front of me, I slackened speed more than they had. I had chains on my tires, and I pumped the brakes repeatedly, enabling me to stop before falling into the depths below. Our three-quarter ton medical truck was close behind me, and was unable to stop before striking me in the rear. Luckily, my jeep avoided being bumped from the road, and at the moment of impact I saw the chaplain's helmet fly to the rear of the jeep. I recall laughing at this, and then noticed that my helmet, too, was thrown into the back seat. Fortunately, our helmets rather than our heads reacted to whiplash.

The trip to Colmar was a long one, and I drove one leg of the journey for twenty-four hours without letup, except for the customary ten-minute break every hour. I was exhausted, and felt myself dozing off. The other drivers in the convoy were able to rest when their assistants took the wheel to relieve them. The officers, too, drove so that their drivers could nap. Chaplain Morgan, however, said that it was not his job to drive. He covered his head with a blanket to keep warm, and smoked cigarettes constantly. The blanket was also necessary to hide the flame from his Zippo lighter and the glow of the burning cigarette. I, too, wanted a cigarette, but had no opportunity to smoke. I told him that I was going to fall asleep and drive off the road if I didn't get relief. He finally, although reluctantly, agreed to get behind the wheel.

Because of the snow, the rough road, the hills, and the loaded trailer, it was necessary to shift the three gear levers often, utilizing front wheel drive and the low range transfer case transmission. The chaplain knew nothing about such shifting of the gears, so the engine would stall, and he was unable to keep up with the convoy. Morgan's ineptitude as a driver, and poor visibility, caused us to leave the road and plow into a high mound of snow. The rest of the convoy passed us and continued on, but the motor pool truck—which was the last vehicle in the convoy—stopped to pull us back on to the road. My old nemesis, the motor pool sergeant, told me to get my rope. It was stowed under the back seat of the jeep, and inaccessible because of all kinds of stuff piled on top of it. I unloaded everything, dumping it on the road beside the jeep until I extricated the rope. I attached it to the jeep, and the truck pulled us back on the road. The towrope was removed and the truck continued on its way; then I piled all of our belongings back into the jeep.

The weather continued to get worse, and I resumed the driving despite being exhausted, because it was evident that the chaplain was incapable of doing so. The only lights available were the blackout lights, which were mere slits in the painted-over headlights. They enabled other oncoming vehicles to see us, but they were inadequate for illuminating the road.

I drove as fast as I could, trying to join the convoy that was out of sight by this time. We drove on and on, but saw no convoy. We came to a fork in the road, and there were tire tracks leading in each direction. I chose an arbitrary set of them to follow, and continued for another several miles, until we felt that we ought to have encountered our troops by this time. The chaplain told me to go back and take the other fork in the road. Our road was narrow, and I could not make a U-turn with the trailer attached, nor was I able to back up and change direction. Knowing that military rank and discipline should be observed, I nonetheless told the chaplain, in a demanding tone of voice, to help me unhitch the trailer, turn it around by hand, and reconnect it. He did so without hesitation realizing, no doubt, the hopelessness of our situation if he did not assist me.

Returning to the other fork in the road, I raced on as fast as I could under the treacherously slippery conditions, and finally came to a town where the convoy stopped. Just before we arrived, the Germans bombarded the town with mortars, inflicting a number of troops with fatalities. We arrived late, to be sure, but we escaped being possible casualties.

The traveling continued for several more days. Our kitchen trucks needed gasoline for the stoves, and when we came to a temporary halt for the usual ten-minute break, the motor pool truck went to each vehicle and asked for its spare five-gallon gas can to supply the kitchen stoves. Every other driver had already emptied his spare can into his gas tank, but I had not. I had saved it for an emergency, expecting to fill my tank later when we arrived at a fuel depot en route.

The convoy continued on, and after a few miles, my tank was empty, and the jeep sputtered to a halt. Every other driver, having already emptied his spare gas can into his gas tank, had enough fuel to continue. The motor pool truck stopped alongside of us, and we were informed that there was a supply of fuel forty miles distant. We were assured that somebody would return with gas so that we could reach the next town.

It was late at night, but the snow-laden trees could be seen. The chaplain and I sat in the jeep, and we saw the glow of artillery in the distance. Other than the crunch of exploding shells in the distance, it was silent in our immediate surroundings. Now and then we heard strange sounds that resembled footsteps, and the chaplain whispered, "Art, get your gun." I extracted it from the gun rack and held it at the ready. As always, I kept it loaded and cocked with a round in the chamber. After a few more suspicious sounds, we discovered that clumps of snow falling from the tree limbs were causing the noise. We continued waiting for the promised fuel supply for a couple of hours, and we heard an approaching vehicle. Not knowing whether it was friend or foe, I stepped out of the jeep and ducked behind it with my rifle pointed at the oncoming vehicle. It was a jeep from another outfit, and its occupants knew nothing about our expected fuel supply. Another hour or so transpired, and the long-awaited truck came with a full gas can.

During a lull in the fighting, we were told that a shower truck was in the area. This was the first time I had a shower for months, and I was issued a clean uniform, underwear, and socks. The shower truck was an ingenious contrivance that held a large tank of hot water and a row of showerheads that could accommodate several men simultaneously. Certainly, a shower seems nothing special about which to write; but after having been unwashed, unshaven, and without a change of clothes for such an extended period, it was as deliriously pleasant an experience as one could possibly imagine. During the Colmar campaign, our division was under the command of the French First Army. We were told that this was the only time American forces were under foreign leadership. The men of this unit were French foreign legionnaires, long-time veterans who served in Africa. They wore fezzes, and insignias identifying them as foreign legionnaires. One of these warriors pointed proudly to the decoration on his uniform and said, "When the Boche see this, they don't take us prisoners, and they know we don't take them prisoners."

These soldiers were constantly inebriated, and in a perpetual state of revelry. They apparently drank no water; their five-gallon water cans were filled with wine. Their behavior was absolutely wanton; they shot animals and chickens at will, and stole anything that wasn't fastened down. They exercised no caution when entering hostile surroundings, and drove into enemy territory at night with headlights lit.

These warriors treated us like long-lost brothers. One of our medics told one of them that the medical truck was overloaded, and more space was needed for equipment and loot. The legionnaire said that he could procure a truck without any difficulty, and suggested that a halftrack might be to our liking. When he said that he would steal the halftrack from another American unit, the offer was rejected.

Chapter 25

Rhine Crossing

The division's contacts with the Germans were, up to this time, in France, Netherlands, Belgium, and Luxemburg. Now it was time to enter the Fatherland and squeeze them until there was nowhere to retreat. Other divisions occupied staging areas up and down the Rhine River for the inevitable invasion of Germany itself. Our division assembled along a levee directly opposite the Ruhr district that was the heart of the enemy's steel industry.

Having little to do until ordered to cross the Rhine, we played touch football every day. Despite the potential danger from snipers on the other side of the river, we felt no great threat, because we were probably a thousand yards distant, and when playing the game, we were constantly on the move, so that we were not satisfactory targets.

Our meals were prepared in the kitchen truck, and we ate from our mess kits outdoors. One day while eating lunch—I still remember that it included chicken a la king—I sat in a corner of a barn and thought the meal to be the best-tasting food I had eaten for months. Suddenly, there was an artillery barrage that zeroed in on us. Undoubtedly, we had congregated too closely together, and presented a temptation for enemy cannons.

Everybody "hit the dirt" as the shells bombarded us, causing some casualties. The delicious meal instantly lost its savor, and I became suddenly sick. The experience confirmed for me that appetite is a function of one's psychological frame of mind.

There was a radio antenna on a rooftop on the other side of the river. We seemed always to have plenty of ammunition, and a mortar squad attempted to destroy the protruding aerial. It was a challenge to hit so small a target, and the squad must have fired a hundred rounds before finally knocking it from the building.

Every night a lone German observation plane, dubbed "Bed Check Charlie," flew reconnaissance over our troops' dug-in positions. The Germans destroyed some bridges crossing the Rhine, and our engineers erected pontoon bridges to replace them. One night, Bed Check Charlie flew his plane a few feet above the river and headed for our bridge. I saw him as he cut his engine on the approach, then, at the last moment, fired his machine guns at the bridge, and gunned the engine as he climbed again into the sky. Moments later he repeated this procedure; then he tried it for the third time, but our anti-aircraft batteries were waiting. As he made his run, opening fire on the bridge, he was shot down, and plunged into the river.

My close friend, Ward Brunner, whom I mentioned earlier, was promoted to sergeant when his squad leader was killed. Ward asked me whether I could spare any razor blades because his supply ran out. I had a full package of extra blades that I gave him, and I thought at the time that, given his perilous job as leader of a machine gun squad, the likelihood of his using the whole package was dubious.

As time for our division to cross the Rhine drew near, the soldiers that were on the river's edge were told to be on the alert for possible German patrols that might land surreptitiously in our midst. Orders were given to shoot on sight anyone seen on the river's bank. Brunner was trying to use a telephone, and the line was dead. Thinking that a wire might be severed, he left his foxhole and crept out to locate the possible break, hoping to repair it. One of his men spotted the movement and, assuming it was an enemy soldier, fired his .30-caliber carbine at the movement. Instantly, Ward hollered, "Don't shoot! It's me, Brunner!" Without reacting quickly to Brunner's alarm, another shot was fired, downing him.

I was in the aid station at the time, and left my rifle outside, because I thought there was no imminent danger of German soldiers being in the area. Brunner was carried into the aid station, and I looked at him, not recognizing his face. The doctor gave him a perfunctory glance, and declared that he was dead. I looked at his dog tags and was shocked beyond belief to see my friend, lifeless. The bullet was not nearly as potent as that from a regular M1 rifle, but it went completely through Ward's chest, exiting on the other side. The doctor said that the speed of the bullet, traveling as close as it did past the heart, was capable of creating enough shock to stop the heart.

My premonition of Ward's not being able to use all of the razor blades that I gave him came true. I know that this omen had nothing to do with Ward's demise, but for a long time I felt guilty for sensing the unlikelihood of his survival.

The wait to cross into Germany's homeland was over. To soften the enemy in preparation for the attack, we were told that artillery batteries belonging to numerous units would be laying a barrage of unprecedented size on the enemy. Many troops had found houses in which to stay while waiting near the riverbank, and I was among them. The warning was given to go into the cellars—or at least vacate the upper floors—for the artillery attack that was about to get underway.

Fifteen hundred artillery pieces, including 105-millimeter howitzers, 155-millimeter long toms, and 240-millimeter cannons, let loose without letup for two solid hours. I took the advice and went down into the cellar. What a phenomenal bombardment! It was like an unceasing roar of thunderous machine guns. One of the artillery rounds had a proximity fuse that caused it to detonate twenty feet above our house and destroy the roof. The next day I saw a piece of the fuse mechanism alongside the house, and when it was shown to an artillery officer, he acknowledged it to be from a 240-millimeter round.

We crossed into Germany on a pontoon bridge constructed by army engineers, and one of my tire chains became stuck in the steel grid of the bridge, and broke off. I was unaware of the loss, and as I continued driving, soldiers who were walking along the road were hollering at me and gesturing with their arms. I thought that they were giving me a big "hello," but after a while I smelled rubber burning, and discovered that a rear tire was flat. It caught fire from being driven on in that condition for a long time. My old antagonist, the motor sergeant, told me how stupid anyone would have to be not to recognize when a flat tire occurred. I told him that I would have detected it had it been a front tire, or if I were not towing a trailer. He declared that the cost of replacing the tire would be deducted from my pay. Such a trivial matter would likely not have great priority for a court-martial, and it was never pursued.

Although Germans were the enemy, I did not hate them. Many times I gave captured soldiers some of my cigarettes, or food if they were hungry. One of the medics, Sergeant Powers, utterly despised the Germans, soldiers and civilians alike. Whenever the medical detachment would set up an aid station in a German home, Powers would deliberately destroy anything for which he had no need, with the intention of making it unusable for the owner, whenever he might return. He would tear up photographs, especially those of uniformed military personnel, and break dishes, furniture, and whatever else available.

At one of the homes were two chairs made of stag horn. They were extremely heavy, and solidly constructed. Powers picked up a chair and slammed it to the ground, with the intention of breaking it apart. The impact did no damage whatsoever. He tried again and again, and was still unable to destroy it. There was an axe nearby, and he attempted to hack it to pieces, but it remained intact. He became so angry in his frustration that he spent hours digging a huge hole in the yard, and buried both chairs out of sight.

In another town, when the aid station was being set up, Sergeant Powers cleared items from a table to be used for medical equipment and medicines. Rather than removing the items in an orderly fashion, he swept them off with the fling of his arm, and detonated a booby trap that was left there by the retreating Germans. I was in the adjoining room and heard a tremendous explosion, having no idea as to its cause. Powers received several wounds from flying shrapnel, but none of the injuries were serious. As he was medicated and bandaged by the doctor, he vilified the Germans in a string of profanities that would be unmatched anywhere. He was the first one from the medical detachment to receive the Purple Heart.

The chaplain and the battalion surgeon were fellow officers who did favors for one another. The chaplain gave his liquor ration to the surgeon in exchange for cigarettes. On one occasion, the surgeon gave several choice steaks—I have no idea from where they came—to the chaplain. The chaplain told me to cook up a couple of them, and I was anticipating what a treat this would be, inasmuch as nearly all of our food was canned "C" rations, "K" rations in cartons, or the infamous "D" bar—a hard, concentrated block of chocolate intended as an emergency energy food source.

The chaplain told me to wrap up the other steaks for later use. The aroma of sizzling meat was glorious beyond measure! When they were done, the chaplain ate both of them, and offered me none. Later, he told me to cook the remaining steaks, and he ate those also by himself.

Chapter 26

End in Sight

I dug no fox holes during combat, although I dug plenty of them during training in the States. I was often in a billet of some sort at night when I was staying with I&R. There were times, however, when I was en route to a new location with the jeep, and was with neither the chaplain nor I&R. In such cases I would try to sleep while sitting in my jeep, or seek a spot that could protect me from mortar or artillery attack. I remember sleeping in the corner of a bombed-out farmhouse, using the rubble of broken stones as a pillow to elevate my head. The hard, rough surface did not bother me because I slept in my helmet, and its close-fitting liner served well as a cushion.

One night as I was sleeping on the ground in the woods, an artillery barrage from the Germans screamed overhead. By this time I became accustomed to the different sound of shells coming in and going out. These missiles detonated when they struck the treetops, and their metallic fragments showered to the ground. They were referred to, appropriately, as tree bursts. Digging a foxhole was not much protection against them; the only recourse I knew was to lie low and pull my helmet down as far as possible. Shrapnel zinged past as the shells exploded above in the tree limbs, but I was not hit. I should have kept a tally of how many times I escaped wounds from artillery (friendly and enemy), bombs, mortars, and bullets; but by the time I thought of doing so, I was unable to keep track of all of them. Ultimately, there would be little purpose; being *almost* injured does not warrant the Purple Heart, nor does it make one a hero.

One night I was driving in a small convoy that consisted of only a dozen or so vehicles. The circumstances were peculiar, in that just a few jeeps and trucks were ordered to some location—we were seldom told why or where we were being sent any-where—and the lead jeep was driven by the motor pool officer, a captain whose customary place in a convoy was in the rear.

We were close to the German lines, and could see and hear enemy artillery fire through the woods. The road on which we were driving was narrow, and blackout conditions prevented our seeing road details very clearly. Suddenly, we all stopped; the lead jeep drove into a bomb crater in the middle of the road. Instantly, artillery shells began raining down on our position. Everybody got out of his vehicle and ran for shelter to a row of vacated, boarded-up houses by the road. I was clawing at a boarded-up entrance, and somebody hollered to me, "Hey! There's no door there!"

My desperate and futile response was, "I'll make one!" All of us abandoned the vehicles, realizing that the Germans knew we were trapped, and had the road zeroed in. Remembering the near loss of my jeep on the road to Grandmenil, and the P-38 strafing the following day, it seemed now that my good fortune may have run out. I envisioned the obliteration of our entire convoy.

While all of the drivers were seeking cover from the barrage, the captain whose jeep went into the crater, ran back and forth yelling for everyone to get back in the vehicles. Orders are orders; so like automatons we returned to the road. Miraculous! Despite the furor, nothing was hit. "Get these vehicles turned around!" barked the officer. Again, this was reminiscent of my earlier situation where I had to turn my jeep and trailer around by hand. We worked feverishly helping each other change direction, and the convoy dashed for safety without a casualty.

A few weeks earlier when it was still winter, and there seemed to be no end of the war in sight, I spoke with German prisoners who expressed confidence that the war would end within a month. They recognized, more than we did, the ultimate futility of continued fighting. As one prisoner told me, "We lost one war; we can lose another."

My most all-consuming, pervasive depression came as a result of having no idea when I would go home again. I said on more than one occasion that I really wouldn't care *when* the war ended if I could be given a specific date, no matter how far distant. One of the fellows said that, no matter how well we did in Europe, fighting was continuing in the Pacific, and the Japanese had to be removed from every island that they occupied. "Do you realize," he said, "that there are islands dotting the whole Pacific Ocean, and how very few we have invaded? We could be at war for another ten or twenty years!" What an absolutely disheartening thought!

As time went on, however, there was a spark of optimism when we began seeing entire companies comprising hundreds upon hundreds of Germans wishing to surrender. One of our other interpreters was born in Germany, and taught me some of the soldiers' songs used to stir their patriotism. When I watched the prisoners of war (POW's) marching back through our lines for incarceration in a stockade, I would sing to them as they passed by, *Heut' gehört uns Deutschland, morgen die ganze Welt.* (Today Germany belongs to us, tomorrow the whole world.) Another favorite was, *O wir fahren gegend England.* (O we're sailing against England.)

Whenever the POW's were marched to the stockade, a couple of riflemen walked alongside or behind them as escort guards. As one group trudged along an icy road, one of the guards slipped and stumbled, and while doing so, his rifle accidentally fired, and a POW fell dead. Not an utterance was heard, nor change of pace. No prisoner so much as turned his head; no one realized it was an accident. We learned later through interrogation that all the POW's believed they were to be systematically executed. By this time everybody on both sides had heard about Malmedy, where German soldiers massacred American soldiers whom they captured, and the German POW's believed they would be victims of reprisal.

Chapter 27

Occupation

Our prime function as assault troops was set aside as other units continued into Germany's heartland until the foe's final surrender. Our division was establishing military governments in towns near Cologne and Düsseldorf. German troops were no longer there, but our military authorities continued to exercise caution in case insurgents might still be able to threaten us.

I was sent from one town to another to act as interpreter for military government personnel. The town crier would call all of its citizens to assemble in the town square, and I stood in their midst telling them what they were, and were not, permitted to do. For instance, I said that they would be able to have funeral processions through the streets as used to be their custom. Before, when the allied bombing occurred, it was unsafe to congregate on the streets, because the mourners became victims of these air raids. I also told the populace the various locations where they would be given food and clothing.

Author conversing with German civilians.

The clergy were also called together, and I informed them that they were allowed in their pulpits, and could teach from the Bible, but would not be permitted to sermonize about political issues. These ministers expressed joy upon hearing this, because when their Nazi regime was in control, they were forbidden to preach a Christian message.

I knew that battles were continuing to rage farther east, and felt fortunate to have my present relatively hazard-free location and assignment. To be certain that our occupation force was secure, a strict curfew was established. I served on this detail every night in the town of Habing-Horst, where I had been weeks before when the town was under siege. Our patrol consisted of four armed soldiers who rode in a jeep through the streets after dark, making sure that no civilians were outside their homes.

Our vehicles still used only blackout headlights, mere slits that provided inadequate illumination for seeing the road. One night as we were making the rounds, our jeep—I was not driving—went into a bomb crater with its front wheels going over the edge. The jeep hung up with its front wheels in the crater and the rear wheels on the street. All of us were thrown from the seats and landed in the hole, but none of us were hurt. At that moment we heard someone opening a window in a nearby house, and I expected to be a target for a sniper lurking somewhere in the darkness, especially since our rifles were dislodged from our hands upon impact. Whoever opened the window meant us no harm, and we walked back to headquarters. Our jeep's drive shaft was damaged, and a truck was sent to pull it from the crater.

One reason that I remember Habing-Horst is that we were shown the moving picture, *A Song to Remember,* featuring Cornel Wild, in a not-too-convincing portrayal of the life of Chopin. The actual pianist who played the piano was Jose Iturbi, one of the leading concert performers and a movie star of the 1940's.

I was now on frequent call by the chaplain to help him with worship services. We made our headquarters in Lüdenscheid, and traveled regularly to several of the other charming burgs nearby. Now that we were again in civilization, the religious services were held in the town's churches. It was an especially happy experience for me, because good pipe organs were always available. This area was not the scene of significant military engagements, and the churches and our billets were largely undamaged.

The army imposed a strict "non-fraternization" policy that prohibited U.S. servicemen from associating, or even speaking, to German civilians. As an official interpreter, I was not under this constraint, and a number of the soldiers implored me to act as go-between for setting them up with dates with the German girls. I told them that I was not a pimp, and they would have to risk getting their own dates.

During the course of official interrogation sessions I heard the Germans denounce their former regime, and no one ever admitted to being a Nazi. When I asked them where all of the Nazis were, they offered no reasonable explanation.

The weather was pleasant, and we formed a chow line outside a home that was used for our kitchen. After eating, we took our mess kits to be washed in the scalding hot soap and rinse water kettles. There wasn't great waste of food, but there were always some leftovers remaining. Before we emptied the leftovers into the garbage pail, the civilians stood in a line with buckets, and begged us to give them our remaining food. This became a ritual at every meal, and no one objected to donating the unappetizing-looking mess for their use.

The house in which I, along with a dozen or so other men, lived was a beautiful residence. Its owners vacated, and I didn't know where they were. For the first time since leaving Wales, we slept in bona fide beds with sheets and blankets. I found a postcard showing a picture of the house, and the address was printed on the card. I mailed it home to my parents, but like all mail from enlisted men, it was censored. When my mother received it, the name of the address was marked out with ink. She used laundry bleach containing chlorine, and applied it to the censor's ink. The imprinted address, made with carbon-based ink, remained intact, but the ink from the censor's pen disappeared, and my mother knew for the first time in months where I was. All during hostilities she read and heard news reports about the war, but never knew my specific location.

Author, after hostilities as part of occupational forces. (Notice Combat Infantryman's Badge above pocket on shirt.)

I was in Lüdenscheid when the armistice between Germany and the Allies was declared. From out of nowhere, booze was present. Some of it was, as had been throughout combat, ethyl alcohol pilfered from the medical supplies. It was often mixed with powdered orange drink included in our rations. I was still a non-drinker at the age of twenty, and was the only sober person in town. Even the chaplain relented from his Methodist policy of abstinence, and drank to our victory.

For us, the end of European hostilities was thought to be only a respite until we would be sent to finish the job in the Pacific. We packed our gear and went by convoy to a processing center in France, from where we would be sent to fight the Japanese.

Chapter 28
Biding our Time

Our convoy required several days to reach the camps in France, where we would be outfitted for service in the Pacific. We were not long underway when one of my tires went flat. It took only a few minutes to replace it with the spare, but shortly afterwards, another tire went flat, and I had to repair it. As anyone knows who has removed a tire from its rim, it is hard work, requiring tire irons to pry it off. I took off the tire and patched it with supplies from the motor pool truck, and put it back on the wheel. After a while the same tire was flat again, and a member of the motor pool helped to repair it and replace it on the wheel. During one day's travel I had six flat tires!

In that era, there were no tubeless tires. Rather, tires were composed of inner tubes that were inserted into outer casings ribbed for traction. With each puncture of my tire, we followed the normal process of locating the hole in the inner tube, scraping the area around it with a rasp, applying adhesive cement, and pressing the rubber patch over the hole. After the sixth flat tire, I examined the outer casing and noticed that it still contained a broken piece of metal—a shard of shrapnel—that was not detected earlier, and every time the repaired inner tube was inserted, it was pierced again. As I expected, the motor pool sergeant began to give me a tongue lashing, but his tirade abated when I told him that one of his crew also overlooked the bit of metal that was still in the casing.

We reached our destination, with different elements of our division going to a number of tent cities near the city of Reims. Most of the camps were named after brands of American cigarettes—Camel, Chesterfield, Lucky Strike—but my battalion was assigned to Camp Washington, an abandoned air strip that our bombers used when making their raids on Germany.

My tent was on Gilbert Street, named as a memorial after Private Gilbert, my friend whom I mentioned earlier as having been killed by a hand grenade tossed into his jeep by a German tank crewman.

These were lazy days with no responsibilities. The men spent their time "shooting the breeze," playing cards, gambling, visiting a Red Cross unit that provided free coffee and doughnuts, and attending movies provided by special services.

Author on leave from Camp Washington

To keep servicemen occupied until they were to ship out for further duty, the European Theater Olympics was organized. American servicemen were invited to compete in athletic competition that, after elimination at battalion, regiment, division, corps, and army levels, culminated in a final tournament at Nürnberg Stadium in Germany.

The same kinds of athletic events that took place in the international Olympic event every four years—postponed during the war—were featured in the military's European Theater version. As noted earlier, archery was one sport at which I demonstrated a degree of expertise; so I applied as a contestant. It was inconceivable to me at the time that our special services branch could provide sports equipment for such diverse athletic events.

We were given lemonwood bows of quite good, though not professional, quality, and a good selection of arrows. Some of the guys who wanted to be competitors were clearly tyros who shot instinctively, but knew nothing about using bow sights or the point-of-aim method demanded for accuracy. Several elimination matches took place until the best shooters were selected for the division team of three archers.

This team went by truck to Chalons to compete at corps level comprising several divisions. All of the teams had an adequate supply of bows, arrows, extra bowstrings, targets, leather armguards and finger guards, but nobody had straw bales on which to fasten the targets. Several team members scouted the countryside, hoping that local farmers could provide us with straw.

None of us spoke enough French to know the word for "straw," nor did anyone know French archery terminology. We didn't think to bring archery equipment with us to show the farmers why we needed straw, so I went through the make-believe motions of shooting a bow and arrow, and our request was understood.

I won the individual title in the semifinal match, and went with our team to the finals in Nürnberg. It was far enough distant to warrant sending us by airplane. I never flew before, and was eager for the new adventure. I had no qualms about flying, but knew that my mother and father had serious misgivings about anything related to aviation. If the plane were to crash, I didn't want my parents to think that I lost my life for a fanciful whim. I wrote a letter to them, stating that I was obligated to go in an airplane, and there was no alternative method of transportation.

The aircraft was a C-47 transport. A row of seats facing another on the opposite side of the aisle was the same configuration used for transporting paratroops. Every seat was occupied, and the cargo compartment was loaded with sports equipment of all kinds. The plane was overloaded, and we were told not to fasten seatbelts. Instead, we had to go to the front near the flight deck and lie on top of each other in order to prevent the plane from being tail-heavy. If this accommodation were not made, the plane would be unable to lift off. We were on a makeshift runway paved with corrugated metal plates. As the twin engines roared during takeoff, we were told facetiously to help get off the ground by grunting, and after reaching

Author (right) with archery team before boarding C-47 transport on the way to European Theater Olympics.

cruising altitude, we resumed our seats.

The stadium at Nürnberg is where the huge rallies of the Nazi party were held when Hitler was in power. It is an impressive facility where the international Olympic Games had been hosted a few years earlier. After finishing each day's archery practice in the stadium, we toured the old city, which was surrounded by a formidable wall with imposing towers.

American athletes from the army and navy who were stationed in Europe participated, and there were many competitors for all of the events. Unlike the semifinal corps playoffs at which individual winners were recognized, team winners only were acknowledged. Our team won third place, and each member received a certificate of congratulation signed by General Dwight D. Eisenhower, rather than the traditional bronze medal.

On the day following the tournament, the Stars and Stripes newspaper announced the dropping of a bomb on Hiroshima that was the equivalent of twenty thousand tons of TNT. Those who read the article were incredulous, and thought the report to be a hoax. That evening there was a USO show in the city featuring Bob Hope, but I didn't go. No public transportation was yet available, and the arena was farther than I wanted to walk. The next day we heard more reports of the mysterious super weapon, and details seemed to make it more credible. We went by truck to Munich to board the airplane to take us back to France, and within a few days the war with Japan was at an end.

There seemed to be a tendency always to look

at the gloomy side of every situation, no matter what the circumstances. While I was in the infantry, the rumor persisted that we would be the last in service to be discharged because we would be needed as occupation forces for years after everybody else went home. When in the MP's, everyone was led to believe that they would remain overseas to maintain order as the conquered nations, Germany and Japan, were learning how to live under democracy. When I was in a finance detachment a year earlier, we were told that we would be required to stay longer than anyone else, because whoever remained would have to be paid, and this would be our obligation.

No one was deluded into thinking that discharge from the military was imminent. With this sentiment ensconced in my mind, I welcomed the news that I, with others who participated in the European Theater Olympics, was eligible for a furlough to the French Riviera. The officers were being sent to Cannes, and the enlisted men would go to Nice. We were taken in the back of an army two-and-one-half ton truck, sitting on wooden benches for the two-day, six hundred mile journey. The ride was miserably uncomfortable, and the truck was covered with a canvas top as protection from the wind and sun. We could look out the back, and see only the scenery that was behind us. Arriving at this noted Mediterranean resort was, however, a treat, especially because it was warm, and warmth was for me an essential, because I was deprived of it for such a long time while being shot at.

We were taken to a pleasant, but modest hotel. In the lobby were slot machines, and I had never seen one-armed-bandits before, nor did I see in real life— but only in the movies back home—a self-service elevator with an open cage like that in our hotel. I felt like a kid, operating this do-it-yourself mechanism. Each room contained a bidet, the purpose for which I did not know at the time. Mirrors were on the ceiling and walls, but I hasten to add that, despite such accoutrements, the establishment was not a brothel.

The ocean looked inviting, so I rented a pair of swim trunks and went to the beach. Women's swimsuits were not yet known as "Bikinis," since no one had heard of Pacific atolls as test sites for nuclear weapons. Their styles, however, were as extreme in their scantiness as is commonplace today; and for us back then, they were truly outrageous. Back in New Jersey, where I went frequently to the seashore, beaches were fine white sand. Here in Nice they were completely made up of stones the size of chicken eggs. We were told that the beach at Cannes, where the officers went for their furlough, was not stony; but it was off-limits to enlisted men.

As a civilian I never saw palm trees, having never been to the tropics, or even to Florida or California, and I took great delight in being in such an environment for the first time. The Negresco was one of the posh hotels in Nice. It looked inviting, so a few of us went to see how rich people spent their vacations. Everyone was dressed "to the nines," and the furnishings were sumptuous.

At a table in the lobby was a sign identifying a man who was sitting there as the then-current chess champion of France. He was waiting for anyone to play with him, and seeing that he had no challengers, I volunteered to be an opponent. I was surprised that there was no charge for playing with him. A few onlookers watched us play, and made no effort to take their turn in playing. The chess grandmaster was a chain smoker, and asked me for cigarettes as we played. We played for several hours, and I gave him a couple of packs. I returned again on subsequent days, and he was always happy to see me.

We played a number of games that were quite lengthy, and I thought that I might win some of them because I was at times a couple of major pieces ahead. Even after he sacrificed, say, a rook and a bishop or a knight, his mastery of the game was so formidable, that I lost every time.

Leaving such pleasant surroundings and the lovely climate, only to return to army life, would normally be difficult to accept; but with peace an actuality, and with the prospect of soon becoming a civilian again, going back to camp was bearable.

Chapter 29
Military Police

Everyone counted his "points" earned for length of service, time in combat, campaign medals, and the like, to estimate when he would be discharged from service. I accumulated sixty points, and if I had had an additional five points for the Purple Heart that my leg wound might have entitled me, I would have been soon on my way home. As it was, I could only wait around, doing nothing important until notified to return to civilian life.

One of my closest friends was Mike Neumann, who was the most recent replacement in the I&R platoon during combat. He was a Jew born in Germany, who left his country with his mother when it became apparent that he would become a statistic of Hitler's purge. Mike told me how, as a child, he thrilled at seeing the proud tank crews in parade, and he wished that he could belong to such an elite group as the Nazi party. He said that his father was a psychiatrist and was actually called upon to examine Hitler during one of his aberrant mental episodes. When it was revealed that his father was Jewish, he "disappeared," and Mike and his mother came to America. He worked as a set designer for Columbia Pictures, and his mother owned an exclusive boutique in Manhattan.

It was ironic that Mike, the newest member of I&R, was the only one to receive the Purple Heart. I saw him as he returned from a mission, and one of his front teeth was missing. He reported to the aid station, saying that a piece of shrapnel struck him in the mouth, breaking off the tooth. His colleagues regarded him as a hero and congratulated him for the medal; and of course it contributed to his point count towards army discharge. Shortly after receiving his Purple Heart, Mike told that me he wasn't hit by shrapnel. Rather, he stumbled while walking up the steps of a house, and fell on his face, breaking his tooth.

As already noted, most of us did nothing constructive to pass our time while in Camp Washington, but Mike volunteered to join the military police detachment that was stationed on the base. He told me that the duty was more gratifying than working for the quartermaster or being a truck driver, jobs to which some of the soldiers were being assigned. These kinds of duties did not appeal to me either, so I went to the provost marshal, asking whether I could join his detachment. He indeed needed more personnel, and welcomed me, making me a special investigator. I no longer carried a rifle, having turned it in when I left my duties with the chaplain to participate in the Olympics. Now I was issued a .45-caliber semiautomatic pistol, and wore an MP brassard on my arm.

This was without doubt the most gratifying experience I ever had since entering the army. Every day and every night brought new and exciting challenges. The MP's usually operated in pairs for their personal security. I went on stakeouts, taking black marketers into custody. I went in a jeep equipped with a siren, and a prominent "Military Police" label painted on the front, to pursue military vehicles that were speeding on the post or on the nearby highways. I went to scenes of vehicular accidents, some of which involved fatalities.

Our detachment had a Harley-Davidson motorcycle, and I was eager to drive it. The provost marshal showed me how to operate the hand gearshift and foot clutch, a transmission system no longer in use today, and he admonished me not to turn up the throttle too suddenly lest the motorcycle take off, leaving me behind. There was also a hand control for advancing or retarding the ignition spark that enabled the engine to run efficiently, and prevented the kickstarter from breaking the rider's leg.

After a few practice sessions on the motorcycle I was given a pouch containing a payroll to be delivered to one of the towns nearby. There were instances reported of highwaymen accosting lone individuals, making such duty potentially hazardous, but I undertook it with enthusiasm.

When the provost marshal learned that I did typing as a chaplain's assistant, he changed my duties to that of a clerk, and I found this work to be irksome. One of the MP's with whom I had worked as an investigator told me to accept this new duty without complaint. He explained—and it was wise advice—that winter was approaching, and being out on a motorcycle would be unpleasant. Being in a warm office, working as a clerk, would be an enviable duty. Validating his argument, he mentioned one of the other MP's whom I knew who rode the motorcycle, and it skidded on gravel, throwing him to the road. He suffered a broken jaw and was taken to the hospital where he had the jaw wired shut. He was unable to eat or drink, except through a straw.

Directly under the provost marshal was the first sergeant, who assigned the men to street patrols, guardhouse, desk sergeant duty, and the like. The provost sergeant was the chief executive in charge of overall operations, and was directly responsible to the provost marshal by the name of Captain McConnell.

The provost sergeant, whom I shall refer to merely as "Joe," was sweet on a French girl, named Yvonne, who worked for us as telephone operator and interpreter. Her role was important because calls came in regarding encounters between American GI's and civilians, and she was able to tell us the civilians' sides of the stories.

Anyone who took an army vehicle off the post was required to have a trip ticket authorizing him to do so. All trucks and jeeps had a rack that held a spare gas can, but no one was allowed to leave the post with a gas can containing fuel. It was assumed that no trip was far enough to warrant carrying the extra gas. Not allowing extra gas to leave the post also prevented its being sold on the black market to civilians, with the soldiers pocketing the proceeds. All vehicles leaving or entering camp were stopped by MP's at any one of several gates of the fenced-in camp. If anyone took a can of gas from the camp, it was impounded at the gate and stored in the back room of the police station. We noticed that these cans in storage were empty, but were full when brought in. Yvonne drove her automobile to the office, and McConnell suspected that Joe was emptying the cans into Yvonne's car.

Rather than confronting Joe or Yvonne, McConnell told me to fill some of the empty cans with water. When Yvonne left the office to go home, the captain and I followed discreetly behind her, and her car sputtered and stalled before she went very far. Unable to explain her predicament satisfactorily, she left the job.

Joe's complicity was obvious, but rather than having criminal charges made against him, he was demoted in rank. A secondary consequence was his being left in Camp Washington when our detachment was transferred a few miles away to the town of Laon. I was given his job in this new location, and promoted from technician fifth grade (corporal) to staff sergeant.

Laon was the ancient capital of France, and situated conspicuously atop a promontory rising from the plain. Our MP station occupied a building at the town's main square, next door to the civilian police department. Not long after moving from Camp Washington to Laon, Captain McConnell was replaced by a new provost marshal, Lieutenant Hobbs. I got along very well with both officers. They allowed me to handle every situation at my own discretion, and never attempted to usurp my authority. I sometimes worked sixteen-hour days, and enjoyed every moment.

Author as provost sergeant.

A few miles from town was a German prisoner of war stockade identified as E-511. Although the war was over, not many American soldiers were being sent home, and German prisoners in custody were not released to go to their homes. The stockade was a barbed wire enclosure, and security was lax. Every few days one or more prisoners made their escape and tried to flee undetected across open farmland. Invariably, a French civilian farmer would see them and recapture them, using a pitchfork or some other tool as a weapon, and the fugitives rarely resisted. Presumably, they figured it was smarter to be taken back to the stockade, rather than risk being killed by refusing to return. The farmer would notify our MP facility, and we would bring the prisoners to our station. Someone would then take them from us and send them to another, more secure detention center elsewhere.

Two escapees were brought to the station early one morning, and I talked with them for a while. They said that under the rules of war, they were entitled to attempt to escape, and they did nothing wrong. They said that they wanted to be home for Christmas. I admit to being angry with them, and said, "*You* want to be home for Christmas! *I* want to be home for Christmas, and it is because of you that I have to be here at all!" I left them sitting there and continued with the day's work. Much later in the day Lieutenant Hobbs stopped at the station to inquire how things were going, and I told him that I was waiting for someone to pick up the escaped POW's. Hobbs asked me when they had eaten anything, and I said that I didn't know; I didn't give them anything. The lieutenant exploded with an expletive of some sort and reprimanded me by saying, "You have to feed these men!"

All three meals of the day had already been served, and the dining hall, located a few blocks way, was closed. Some doughnuts were on a table, and I offered them to the prisoners. It was pathetic to see them wolf them down so ravenously, and there was no coffee to go with them. I felt really troubled by my thoughtlessness, for I remembered treating prisoners just taken in battle more humanely.

Laon attracted American soldiers on pass who frequented several of the cafes that sold alcoholic beverages. We had no jurisdiction over the French civilians, but advised them that only wine or Champaign, rather than hard liquor, be served in their drinking establishments. There was a genuine effort made to comply with this request, but GI's often became belligerent, starting fights and damaging the premises. When this kind of problem arose, I told my men to take truncheons and helmets to quell such disturbances.

I was on duty seven days a week, and there was only a skeleton crew on Sundays. One Sunday morning I received a call that there was a soldier who was AWOL, and that he was reported as being at the train depot. His commanding officer asked my help in apprehending him. He said that the runaway was black, and could be easily recognized, since there were few colored soldiers in the vicinity. I took the jeep and drove to the station. No trains were there, and the platform was isolated except for one black soldier. I called to him and he started to run. When I drew my pistol from its holster, he said, "Okay, okay. Don't shoot!" He came to me peaceably, and I took him back to the station. Whenever I drove someone that I arrested, and if we were alone, I rotated my pistol belt so that the weapon was on my left, out of his reach.

On another Sunday, when there was no one else in the station except the desk sergeant and me, I heard a disturbance outside. Two paratroopers from the 82nd Airborne Division, on a weekend pass, knocked over a "No Parking" sign that was on the curb just outside of our building. I went out and told them to put the sign back where it had been. The 82nd was universally admired for its heroism, but its members had the reputation of being cocky, and were known to intimidate members of other units. The men laughed derisively, and asked who was going to make them do it. I hollered for the desk sergeant to come out. He was a strong, gangly, hillbilly-type from Mississippi. I told him what happened, and he said to the paratroopers, "You guys think you're tough! We'll find out how tough you really are! There are two of you and there are two of us. Put the sign back!" When the perpetrators recognized that we were not going to be bullied, and saw that we were armed with .45's, they complied without further confrontation.

During a French holiday—I forget now what it was—a carnival came to the town square. There were amusement rides and other typical carnival entertainment. There was a test of brawn that was determined by one's ability to shove a weighted box on wheels up an inclined track, until it struck an explosive device at the top of its run. Its purpose was a test of strength, similar to that at fairs or carnivals in America where one swings a mallet, and tries to send a projectile high enough to ring a bell.

Several of us from our police station were watching as townspeople attempted to send the weighted box to the top. If one could send it all the way, additional weight was added, and further attempts were made. One after the other, civilians tried to set off the explosion, but after a few kilos of weight were added, the box was unable to reach the top. The Mississippian who helped me confront the paratroopers shortly before, bought a ticket allowing him to try his luck. On his first try, he told the concession operator to add all of the weights that were available. With a mighty push, he sent the load to the very top, setting off the detonation signaling success, a feat that no civilian could equal.

There was never a day—in fact, hardly an hour—that passed by without a situation requiring action by our MP's. Barroom brawls were commonplace. One of the principal attractions in town was the Café Lion Rouge, and its proprietors telephoned us often to remove GI's whose behavior was potentially dangerous to the mirrors and other furnishings. We were called to apprehend a disorderly soldier who was an American Indian. For any situation that might require strong-arm tactics, I usually assigned two of my best men, sergeants Drummond and Mohra. Mohra was a Pennsylvania State Trooper in civilian life, and was adept at handling unruly adversaries. If our office was not overly busy, I would ask the desk sergeant to fill in for me, and I would go with my agents to the scene of action.

When we arrived at the café, the Indian was throwing bottles and behaving like a madman. Mohra and another man grabbed him, one on each arm. I stood facing him, and Drummond was directly behind me. The Indian was a big guy, weighing well over two hundred pounds. With a mighty heave, he wrenched free of both his captors and threw a punch at me. I ducked, and Drummond, who was behind me, was struck in the mouth. All four of us finally subjugated the Indian and took him into custody. We nicknamed Drummond "Liver Lips" because of his swollen mouth.

Whenever we arrested any G.I., we notified his company commander, who was required to take him back for whatever disciplinary action that was warranted. Our office only apprehended wrongdoers, but had no role in their litigation.

Vehicular accidents were frequent. I once went to investigate a collision between an army truck and a bicycle ridden by a civilian French woman. She was killed outright and her bicycle was completely destroyed, and the only damage to the truck was a small flake of paint that was scratched from the bumper.

Another accident involved a jeep that was reported as having collided with a large tree. When I arrived to examine the circumstances, I saw an inebriated army major sitting in the jeep, which was severely damaged. I asked to see the trip ticket authorizing him to drive the jeep. (All vehicles leaving a

base were required to have this document.) He didn't
have one. When I told him that he was under arrest,
he said that he outranked me, and that he would not
be taken into custody. I knew that my law enforce-
ment role superseded his rank, and told him to get
into my jeep. He drew a pistol from his pocket in his
effort to intimidate me. It was a tiny, nickel-plated,
.22-caliber semiautomatic, and I was able to grab it
from him because of his being in a stupor.

As I escorted him to my jeep, he became doc-
ile, and bemoaned the fact that he could be "busted"
in rank if I turned him in. I took my job seriously, and
knowing that my backing down was out of the question, took him to our office, and he was picked up by
his superior officer. My report charged him with ine-
briation in public, unauthorized use of a vehicle, possession of a concealed weapon, and resisting arrest.
I learned later that he was, indeed, reduced in rank
to 2nd lieutenant, and I was surprised that it actually
happened!

A year transpired since I was in the muddy camp
in Fréville, preparing to confront an actual enemy. I
remembered it as the place where I had my twentieth
birthday. When I told my men it was my twenty-first
birthday, they wanted to celebrate by having a party
at the local Café Lion Rouge, where we had the frequent encounters with troublesome GI's.

A Dutch woman, who worked in town, rented
a room above the café. She was a friend of one of my
MP's, and invited us to have the party at her place.
Everybody was in a festive mood, and the beverage

for the occasion was gin and Coca-Cola. In that era, Coke was distributed in dark green bottles. The procedure for serving the drinks was to pour out a small amount of Coke and replace it with gin. I was offered one of the concoctions, and thought it tasted great. As the evening wore on, I was handed several refills. Since everyone knew that I was not accustomed to imbibing habitually, they thought it would be fun to make me inebriated without my being aware of it. Each successive bottle of coke was emptied more than the previous one, and the Coke replaced with gin. Neither the dark-colored bottle nor any appreciable difference in taste revealed to me that my alcoholic intake was considerable. I was oblivious to later details of my party, and with my return to consciousness, I awakened in my barrack to where I was carried the night before. This was the first and last time I was indisputably drunk!

Chapter 30
Homeward Bound

Another outfit was coming to town to replace us, since we had accumulated enough points towards discharge from the army. I was deliriously happy at the prospects of getting out of service, but regretted only that it took me so long to have military duty that I so thoroughly enjoyed, and in which I had a purposeful and effective impact.

The key to finding gratification in my duties was my being given a semblance of authority, and not being constantly subject to onerous and perilous situations. Another element that provided satisfaction was being exposed to enough potential danger to keep adrenalin high, and yet being in circumstances where I was in control and had the edge in risky confrontations. In contrast, when engaged in real war against a formidable enemy, I felt my chances of survival were few or none at all, and my pleasure in doing my job was less than enthusiastic.

For reasons that I never fully understood, I was assigned to a field artillery unit before being allowed to leave Europe and ultimately be discharged from service. We were transported by truck to a tent city near Le Havre, our port of embarkation. It was cold and snowy, and the tents were heated with little coal stoves. The occupants of a tent a few yards away used gasoline to help ignite a fire more quickly. There was a muffled "poof," and all that remained of the tent were charred timbers.

Not having had a bath for many months, I was eager to use the shower that was available in the camp. I turned on the wonderfully warm water and applied soap, and while washing, the water suddenly turned cold. A German prisoner of war was the fireman with the responsibility of maintaining heat in the boiler, but he neglected to attend to the job properly. I yelled, "Wo ist der Heizer?" (Where is the fireman?) After I hollered several times, the prisoner entered the shower room and, not knowing my rank because I was naked and without rank insignia, saluted and apologized. I didn't want to dry myself with a towel, since I had no opportunity to rinse off the soap, so I shivered and cussed until the water became warm enough to finish satisfactorily.

In our pyramidal tent I managed to select a spot for my cot that was close to the stove. It was so near, in fact, that the wooden spars, over which the canvas was stretched, caught fire, but I extinguished it before my bed fell apart. Not having learned a lesson from the explosion that destroyed a nearby tent a day or so before, one of the men in my tent poured a bottle of gasoline into the stove in which there were a few smoldering ashes. There was an explosion, but rather than destroying our tent, the lid and smokestack of the stove blew off. Fortunately, no injuries occurred.

Despite the gloom and cold of this encampment, our spirits were high, knowing that it would not be long before departure. We went by truck to the port and boarded the Victory ship, U.S.S. Colby. It was one of many such craft built in record time by Henry Kaiser as troop transports. They were cheaply constructed, and a few of them cracked open and sank. The seams in the hull were welded rather than riveted, and resulted in structural failure.

We were at sea for a day, and had to return to Le Havre because the refrigeration system was not operating properly. We concealed our disappointment for the delay by declaring that we enjoyed leaving France so much that we went back to leave it twice.

The sea was exceedingly rough, and I felt nauseated, much as I did when crossing the Atlantic from west to east. Unlike my earlier crossing when I was in a cabin, I slept in the hold on a hammock, in close quarters with men above and below me. As the ship rose and fell with the waves, it shuddered violently when the stern was lifted out of the ocean and the rotating propeller blades struck the water. I touched the inside surface of the hull with my hand, and had some disquieting thoughts about there being no more than a few inches, at most, of fragile metal between me and an entire ocean!

The voyage required ten days. Seasickness in varying degrees affected many of us, but one fellow lay on his hammock without once rising, and ate nothing until his buddies insisted that he eat an apple and sip water periodically to stay alive. His facial color was grayish-green, and he groaned in agony incessantly. I have been seasick on a fishing boat for a couple of hours, and know how hopeless one feels, knowing he can do nothing about his plight until he reaches shore. This poor fellow, having to endure this torment for ten whole days, said he would have shot himself if he were given the opportunity.

Entering New York harbor, we saw the welcoming, upraised arm of the Statue of Liberty, and saw the Queen Mary also arriving into port, carrying British war brides coming to join their new American husbands. Our ship came alongside the pier, and while yet a distance of six feet or so from actually touching it, one of the soldiers on board tossed his duffle bag over the rail, expecting it to land on the dock. Instead, it fell into the water between the ship's hull and the dock. It would have been dangerous to try to retrieve the bag; any such attempt could result in a rescuer's being crushed to death. Not only were all of his belongings such as clothing, and the like, gone, but I could only imagine what items such as souvenir weapons or other valuables were lost forever.

Our next stop was the separation center at Camp Kilmer, where I was stationed a long time ago. We moved into the wondrous comfort of a bona fide, clean, comfortable barrack, and were treated to what everyone agreed was the most spectacularly delicious meal beyond anyone's wildest imagination. The truth is, the meal was very good, but quite prosaic, comprising a juicy, well-done steak, peas, mashed potatoes, rolls, and ice cream. I can still taste it!

A couple of days remained before the discharge documents would be forthcoming, and everyone was admonished to stay in camp. No one was given leave, and anyone found guilty of being AWOL was threatened with having his discharge withheld for an indefinite period. A few of the men whose homes were in the immediate area, and especially if they were married, sneaked out of camp, and of those whom I knew who took the risk, all returned without being detected.

With receipt of our discharge certificate, and the sewing of the "ruptured duck" label—signifying separation from service—on to the lapel of our GI issue overcoat, we bade farewell to our comrades. I took the train from New Brunswick to Philadelphia, a commuter train across the Delaware River, and a bus to West Collingswood. I telephoned home, telling my mother that I was soon to arrive. She went to the store, and was not home when I got there. I saw a neighbor lady next door who did not recognize me, and I went to another neighbor's house to wait until my mother returned. She bewailed not having been home, and expressed deep guilt for not being the first to meet me. Almost immediately I removed my uniform and changed into civilian clothes, something I had not done for almost three years. It was time to live life anew. School, a job, marriage, and whatever else the future promised, all lay ahead.

The End
June 17, 2005

Contact Arthur Birkby
or order more copies of this book at

TATE PUBLISHING, LLC

127 East Trade Center Terrace
Mustang, Oklahoma 73064

(888) 361 - 9473

Tate Publishing, LLC

www.tatepublishing.com